Anunnaki Series

A set of 3 Books

BOOK 2

The Anunnaki and Ulema-Anunnaki Vault of Forbidden Knowledge and the Universe's Greatest Secrets. Book 2

A set of 3 books

Copyright ©2010 by Maximillien de Lafayette. All rights reserved. No part of this book may be used or reproduced by any means, graphic, electronic, or mechanical, including photocopying, recording, taping or by any information storage retrieval system without the written permission of the author except in the case of brief quotations embodied in critical articles and reviews. Date of Publication: May, 2010

The Anunnaki and Ulema-Anunnaki Vault of Forbidden Knowledge and the Universe's Greatest Secrets.
Book 2

A set of 3 books

Maximillien de Lafayette

*** *** ***

Contributions by
Ulema Mordachai ben Zvi
Ulema Kira Yerma
Ulema Ramash Govinda
Master Li

Times Square Press. Elite Associates International

Jamiyat Ramadosh Al-Ulema Al-Anunnaki
New York California London Paris Tokyo

*** *** ***

2010

Acknowledgment and Gratitude

I am deeply grateful to the Honorable Anunnaki-Ulema who have generously contributed to this book:
Contributors:
Master Li
Ulema Sharif Al Mutawalli
Ulema Mordachai Ben Zvi
Ulema Sadik Bin Jaafar Al Kamali
Ulema F. Oppenheimer
Ulema A. Berkof
Ulema Ramash Govinda
Ulema Tabeth Al-Baydani
Ulema Shaul Sorenztein
Sinhar Ambar Anati
Ulema F. Tayara
Ulema Mirach Faridi Beraz
For without their guidance and contributions, this book would have remained stacks of papers in my drawer.

⌘⌘⌘

Table of Contents (Book 2)

38. On activating the Conduit, decontaminating or cleansing ourselves, galactic species in the Milky Way, galaxy and universe, stargates, invasion of Iraq, Anunnaki and extraterrestrial spaceships and UFOs...31
Questions...31
- Question #1: Are the Sumerian gods Enlil, Enki, Inanna and Marduk still alive and will they be returning to earth in 2022 or not? (A question I asked Zechariah Sitchin in person November 2007 but he did not answer)... 31
- Answer of Ulema Maximillien de Lafayette...31
- Question #2: Is it possible for us earth humans to activate our conduit ourselves here on earth, and if so what is the technique to do so...32
- Answer of Ulema Maximillien de Lafayette...32
- Question #3: When will Sinhar Marduchk's notes for 2022 be published?... 33
- Answer of the Anunnaki-Ulema...33
- Question #4: What material / spiritual /lifestyle changes would we need to make in order to decontaminate or cleanse ourselves as much as possible prior to the return in 2022?...33
- Question #5: Is it possible that mind controlling frequencies can be remotely transmitted into our homes through devices such as the cable box or TV or other electronic instruments? Steven Greer's book Hidden Truth, Forbidden Knowledge says yes...33
- Answer of the Anunnaki-Ulema...33

- Question #6: Have you read "Alien Interview"? In it the EBE says she is a member of the Domain Expeditionary Force sent from the Domain to explore, investigate and conquer this part of the galaxy en route to the galactic center, and claim the Domain to be an extremely old and very advanced civilization...34
- Answer of the Anunnaki-Ulema...34
- Question #7: What do the Annunaki have to say about other galactic species, how many are they and how much interaction between species is going on here and elsewhere in the Milky Way galaxy and universe? ...35
- Answer of the Anunnaki-Ulema...35
- Question #8: Is there a stargate in New York City?...36
- Answer of Ulema Maximillien de Lafayette...36
- Question #9: How many stargates exist across the planet?...36
- Answer of the Anunnaki-Ulema...36
- Question #10: Are there specific times when they can be used or are they always open?...37
- Answer of the Anunnaki-Ulema...37
- Question #11: I heard one of the reasons for the illegal invasion of Iraq was to shut down their stargates and the U.S. military has built bases on top of them, as well as building bases over ancient archaeological sites of Anunnaki temples/ libraries/ abodes.) ...37
- Question #12: Do the home planets of extraterrestrials visiting/ inhabiting earth exist in higher dimensions within our own galaxy?...37
- Answer of the Anunnaki-Ulema...38
- Question #13: What is the method of propulsion to travel interdimensionally and what do these ships look like and consist of? ...38
- Answer of the Anunnaki-Ulema...38

- Question #14: What are Anunnaki ships made of and how do they look? ...38
- Answer of the Anunnaki-Ulema...38
- Question #15: What are Anunnaki ships and extraterrestrial crafts made of and how do they look? ...38
- Answer of the Anunnaki-Ulema...38

39. On sharing the same God with extraterrestrials, the great book of knowledge, end of our planet, the truth in the Bible, are the Anunnaki the bad guys?...45

Questions...45
- Question #1: Do we all share the same god? ...45
- Answer of the Anunnaki-Ulema...45
- Question #2: Did they make us? ...45
- Answer of the Anunnaki-Ulema...45
- Question #3: When will we know the full truth? ...45
- Answer of the Anunnaki-Ulema...45
- Question #4: What is man here for? ...45
- Answer of the Anunnaki-Ulema...45
- Question #5: Is there a great book of knowledge?...49
- Answer of the Anunnaki-Ulema...49
- Question #6: When will our planet end? ...49
- Answer of the Anunnaki-Ulema...49
- Question #7: Is the Bible the truth? ...49
- Answer of the Anunnaki-Ulema...49
- Question #8: Why don't they show them self to people who seek? ...49
- Answer of the Anunnaki-Ulema...49
- Question #9: Will humans destroy earth? ...50
- Answer of the Anunnaki-Ulema...50

- Question #10: The Anunnaki are the bad guys, don't you agree? ...50
- Answer of the Ulema...50

40. On the Bando Project, and the study of the anatomy of dead aliens' bodies, and extraterrestrial survivors...53
Questions...53
- 1. What was the purpose of the Bando Project? ...53
- 2. Is this secret project still going on? ...53
- 3. What were the findings and results of the project
- Author's note/answer...53
- Bando Project ...53
- I. Definition and introduction...53
- II. Allegations...53
- III. Former double agent's claims...54
- IV. The Russian newspaper/website Pravda article...54

41. On "Barage Europa" (Extraterrestrial tunnels/structures)...59
- Question: I heard once Mr. de Lafayette talking about Barage Europa. I missed the beginning of his speech. What did he mean by Barage, and is this Barage related to extraterrestrial structures on Europa near Jupiter?... 59
- Ulema de Lafayette's answer...59

42. On Bariya, and the Anunnaki's creation of Man...63
Questions...63

- Question #1: I can't read the Sumerian texts to understand what is going on. I am interested in finding anything that tells me something about how the Anunnaki created us? ...63
- Question #2: Where are those texts? ... 63
- Question #3: And something else, and without any offense to you, please guide me to authors other than the Ulema and your group who have found anything on this...63
- Question #4: And by the way, what did you mean by Bariya? I read about it in one of your books, and could not understand a thing." ...63
- Authors' answers and comments by other scholars...63
- Bariya "Ba-riya'ah" ...63
- I. Definition...63
- II. Bariya (The Creation) as described in the Sumerian texts...63
- III. The creation of humans...64
- Here are additional Akkadian/Sumerian clay tablets passages on the creation of the Man and pertinent comments by scholars, historians, linguists and the authors...64
- Ninlil, the legendary Sumerian "Queen Breeze"
- Marduk was the son of Ea...65
- In the Akkadian/Sumerian epic Enuma Elish, we read...65
- Inanna was the legendary Sumerian goddess who created the first 7 prototypes of mankind...65
- The Sumerian-Anunnaki goddess Nammu "Namma" and her son Enki created multiple forms of humans...66
- Ea killed Kingu, the demon son of Tiamat, and used his blood to create mankind...66
- Apsu and the creation of man... 66
- From the Sixth Tablet...66

- From the Seventh Tablet...66

43. On Mu, Anunnaki's interference in Earth's affairs, the reptilians, departure and return of the Anunnaki, God, religions, and life after death...71

Questions...71
- Question #1: MU's connection with the Anunnaki. What can you tell me about the lost continent of MU? ... 71
- Answer of the Anunnaki-Ulema...71
- Question #2: Where are the Anunnaki right now and why don't they interfere on our planet anymore? ...73
- Answer of the Anunnaki-Ulema...73
- Question #3: We see, nearly every ancient civilization somehow had some sort of contact with the Anunnaki. So what did happen after that?...74
- Where did Anunnaki go and why? ...74
- Answer of the Anunnaki-Ulema...74
- Question #4: Is it true that lots of Earth governments including US are controlled or ruled by an Alien race called reptilians? ...74
- Answer of the Anunnaki-Ulema...74
- Question #5: So, if modern religions are false, is there a God Almighty? ... 74
- Note...74
- Question #6: What does happen to us when we die? ...74
- Note...74
- Question #7: Were the prophets controlled by Anunnaki or they have manipulated the people as they wished? ... 74
- Answer of the Anunnaki-Ulema...74

- Question #8: Do you know anything about old Turks named Gokturks? ...75
- Answer of the Anunnaki-Ulema...75
- Question #9: Do you have any knowledge about Turks and their connection with Anunnaki or Sirius system? ...75
- Answer of the Anunnaki-Ulema...75
- Question #10: In the Lost book of Enki, Zecharia Sitchin wrote, the mysterious face on Mars (which is still unaccepted by NASA) was Anunnaki Alalu's graveyard. Do you know is it true? ...76
- Answer of the Anunnaki-Ulem...76
- Question #11: Are Enlil, Enki, Anu etc. still alive?
- Answer of the authors...76
- Note...76
- Question #12: Can you write some info about you? Where and when did you born, how did you go and learn the ways of the Ulema, etc.? ... 76
- Answer of the authors...76

44. On teleportation (Barka-kirama)...79
Questions...79
- Question #1: What is the technique called Barka-kirama, Anunnaki Ulema use for teleportation? ...79
- Question #2: Please define Barka-kirama...79
- Note... 79
- I. Definition...79
- II. In ancient Middle Eastern literature...79
- III. The concept...80
- IV. The Taj Baba's theory...82
- V. The Tay Al Ard, self-teleportation and concept of the Alkiramat "Keramat"... 82

45. On the various aliens capabilities of learning many languages and ways of using their methods to learn these languages...87
Questions... 87
- Question # 1: How do all the various aliens know so many of our languages? ... 87
- Ulema Maximillien de Lafayette's answer...87
- Question # 2: Is there a way for us to learn using their methods?...91
- Answer...91
- Question# 3: It would make the world a much better place if everyone could understand each other...92
- Answer ...92

46. On super tall beings, Coral Castle, Admiral Byrd, animal mutilations...95
Questions...95
- Question #1: What is known about The Big Boys...the super, super tall beings that are like no other entities?... 95
- Ulema de Lafayette's answer...95
- Question #2: Who were the beings who lived in the caves in the American southwest which were discovered approx. 100 years ago by the Smithsonian explorer?... 96
- Ulema de Lafayette's answer...96
- Question #3: Does Lafayette have any theories as to how 'coral castle' was built? ... 97
- Ulema de Lafayette's answer...97
- Question #4: Does Lafayette have any theories as to the meaning of the crop circles? ... 97
- Ulema de Lafayette's answer...97

- Question #5: What is really going on on the moon? ...98
- Ulema de Lafayette's answer...98
- Question #6: Is there anything to the theories regarding what Admiral Byrd saw from the plane at the South Pole and the reports from places like Mt Shasta? ... 98
- Ulema de Lafayette's answer...98
- Question #7: Who or what is really doing the animal 'mutilations' and for what reason? ...98
- Ulema de Lafayette's answer...98

47. Rekh-get-Amen, and the Anunnaki-Ulema Extraordinary Deeds and Faculties...101

- Definition and introduction...101
- II. Unusual deeds by Anunnaki-Ulema as told by an Ulema novice...101
- 1. Introduction: The Anunnaki-Ulema...101
- a- Anunnaki-Ulema, Grand Master Li...102
- b- Anunnaki-Ulema Cheik Al Huseini...103
- c- Anunnaki-Ulema Rabbi Mordechai...103
- II. Stories about the Anunnaki-Ulema...105
- 1. Master Li calming down a cobra in the street of Benares...105
- 2. Making a bird from paper...106
- 3. Master Li feeding the fish and birds with food that came from nowhere...108
- 4. The Tuareg and the magical coffee cup...110
- 5. Folding the space...115
- 6. The amazing deeds of Anunnaki-Ulema Mordechai...118
- Here are some fabulous stories told by Germain Lumiere who is now visiting Ulema Mordechai in Budapest, Hungary...132

48. Brain "The Supersymetric Mind"...141
Study of the influence of the Anunnaki's programming of our brain and fate...141
- I. Introduction...141
- II. Excerpts from Ulema Sorenztein's Kira'at...142
- III. The Supersymetric Mind...149
- a. A brief note on supersymetry...149
- b. What is a "Supersymetric Mind"? ...149

49. The Duplicate Image or Reproduction of a Being "Ishra"...153
- I. Definition...153
- II. Ulema Mordechai ben Zvi explains...153

50. Apparition of Dead Pets. Communication with our Dead Pets "Gensi-uzuru" ...155
- I. Introduction...155
- II. Is it possible to communicate with our dead pets? ...155
- III. When your departed loved pet returns to see you...156
- IV. Excerpts from Master Li's Kira'at on Gensi-uzuru...158

51. Levels of the Mind "Iama" ...161
- I. Definition and introduction...161
- II. "All humans have more than one brain" ...161

52. Interpretation of Messages Sent to the Conduit "Haridu", "Haridu-ilmu"...163
- I. Definition...163

- II. Ulema Rabbi Mordechai explains Haridu–Conduit Equation ...163

53. Plasmic Halo Surrounding the Physical Body "Hatani"...169
- I. Definition...169
- II. The concept...169
- III. The Hatani "Protection Shield" ...170
- IV. Hatani and Khuch "Kush-Ra": Protection against physical threats and harms...173

54. Shape-shifting "Ibra-Anu" ...177
- I. Definition and introduction...177
- II. Anunnaki's shape-shifting...177

55. Bringing Youth to Your Face. "Hatori-shabah" ...179
- I. Definition...179
- II. Ulema Suleiman Al Bak'r explains the concept...179

56. The Ability of Observing Entities Fluctuation "Idartari" ...181
- I. Definition...181
- II. Pets and children ability to see non-physical entities...181

57. Extraterrestrials in the Book of Ramadosh "Ezakarfalki", "E-zakar-falki"...185

- I. Definition and introduction...185
- II. Evolution of the extraterrestrials and the human races...186
- III. Extraterrestrial races populated the Earth...186
- IV. Extraterrestrials of the sea (Underwater) ...186
- V. Senses of the extraterrestrials...187
- VI. Talking to extraterrestrials...187

58. The First stage of the Afterlife "Hattari"...190
- I. Definition...190
- II. Description...190

59. The Fourth Dimension "Chabkaradi"...195
- I. Definition...195
- II. Explanation...195

60. State of the Human Mind After Death "Zrah-Amru"...199
- I. Definition...199
- II. The Ulema explain...199

61. Anunnaki's Device for Reading and Deciphering Codes and Symbols "Hazi-minzar", "Mnaizar" ...202
- I. Definition...202
- II. Description...202
- III. The text ...202

62. Entities Created by the Anunnaki, and the Ulema in Modern Times "Helama-Gooliim"...211
- I. Definition and introduction...211
- II. Their nature and essence...211
- III. The creation process of these entities...212

63. Folding-Unfolding the Earth "Hiraaba-safri"...215
- Ulema Cheik Al Kabir explained...215

64. Longevity of Quasi-Human-Life Form "Izra-nafar-mikla'ch"...217
- I. Definition...217
- II. The Anunnaki-Ulema explain...217

65. Immortality After Death "Izrahi-ghafra"...219
- I. Definition...219
- II. The Anunnaki-Ulema explain...219

66. Columns "charged" with Anunnaki's Supernatural Powers "Jachim", "Jachin"...222
- Two large cast-bronze pillars in the Temple of Solomon...222
- I. Definition and introduction...222
- II. Ulema's interpretation...222

67. Abbreviation of Yahweh "Jah", "Yah"...225

- I. Definition...225
- II. In Ana'kh/Ulemite literature...225

68. Anunnaki's Sex and Reproduction "Jin.Si-Yah" ...227
- I. Introduction...227
- II. Hybrids...227
- III. Major points about the subject...228

69. Short Mental Projection of the Self "Ka"...229
- I. Definition...229
- II. Ka and the Egyptians...229

70. Multiple Dimensions' Dividing Lines "Kalem" ...231
- Definition...231

71. Center of Energy "Kama"...233
- I. Definition...233
- II. In Hebrew, esoterica and Kabala...233

72. Etheric Manifestation "Karsha-bita"...235
- I. Definition...235
- II. The bird as a symbol of the soul...235

73. Hybrids' Dwellings "Korashag "Khur-Shag"...239

- I. Definition and introduction...239
- II. Description of the hybrids' habitat...239
- a- Human environment...240
- b- Underground/underwater communities...240
- III. Characteristics...240
- Bedrooms, beds, toys, dining rooms, food, and eating habits...241
- IV. Hybrid children habitat as described by an Anunnaki...241
- a. Inside the base...241
- b. The refectory...242
- c. Hybrids' three distinct groups/categories...243
- d. Hybrids placed for adoption...243
- e. Disposing of the food and cleaning the refectory...244
- f. Dormitories and sleeping quarters...244
- g. Attending various activities...245
- h. The fetuses' room...247

74. Physical manifestation of a dead person, before entering another dimension "Kusir and Lalladu" ...249
- 1. Introduction...249
- 2. Kusir and Lalladu...250
- a. Meaning of Kusir...250
- Kusir-Ra...250
- Kusir-Ji...250
- b. Meaning of Lalladu...251

75. Reading Past, Present, and Future Events From the Life of one Single Person "La-abrida", "Bzi'ra-irdu"...261
- 1. Definition and introduction...261

- 2. Synopsis of mode of operation...263
- 3. The beginning of everything; multiples existences and "God's Particle" ...264
- 4. La-abrida "Bzi'ra-irdu"; is it a tool to go back in time or jump into the future? ...266
- Is it a tool to go back in time or jump into the future? ...266
- 5. Can I use La-abrida"Bzi'ra-irdu" to ameliorate my life, and change my destiny? ...267
- 6. Revisiting your childhood in another dimension, in another time...270
- 7. The invisible and thin quantum line dividing two space-time dimensions...274
- 8. Q&A ...276

76. Spathe of the Male Date-Palm "Lagishimmar", "Lagi-zulum"...281
- Also called the deity's hand-bucket...281
- 1. Definition and introduction...281
- 2. Symbolism...283
- 3. Esoteric and magical use...284

77. A tool to Rewind the Past and the Future "Lamada-burkadi"...287
- Definition...287

78. Metaphysical Visual Stethoscope "Lamadru"...289
- Definition...289

79. Announcement of your Death "Latabi", "Ma-ari" ...291

- I. Definition...291
- II. Ulema Al Baydani explains...291

80. The Image of the Bodies of People Who Have Passed Away "Lakur-bashar-shabah", "Mah.Ga.Ri" ...293
- I. Definition...293
- II. Etymology...293

81. Reappearance of Objects which are no longer in Existence...295 Lakur-shabah", "Mah.Ri.Nag"...295
- I. Definition...295
- II. Etymology...295

*** *** ***

38. On activating the Conduit, decontaminating or cleansing ourselves, galactic species in the Milky Way, galaxy and universe, stargates, invasion of Iraq, Anunnaki and extraterrestrial spaceships and UFOs
⌘⌘⌘

- Question #1: Are the Sumerian gods Enlil, Enki, Inanna and Marduk still alive and will they be returning to earth in 2022 or not? (A question I asked Zechariah Sitchin in person November 2007 but he did not answer)
- Answer of the Anunnaki-Ulema
- Question #2: Is it possible for us earth humans to activate our conduit ourselves here on earth, and if so what is the technique to do so
- Answer of the Anunnaki-Ulema
- Question #3: When will Sinhar Marduchk's notes for 2022 be published?
- Answer of the Anunnaki-Ulema
- Question #4: What material / spiritual /lifestyle changes would we need to make in order to decontaminate or cleanse ourselves as much as possible prior to the return in 2022?
- Question #5: Is it possible that mind controlling frequencies can be remotely transmitted into our homes through devices such as the cable box or TV or other electronic instruments? Steven Greer's book Hidden Truth, Forbidden Knowledge says yes
- Answer of the Anunnaki-Ulema

- Question #6: Have you read "Alien Interview"? In it the EBE says she is a member of the Domain Expeditionary Force sent from the Domain to explore, investigate and conquer this part of the galaxy en route to the galactic center, and claim the Domain to be an extremely old and very advanced civilization
- Answer of the Anunnaki-Ulema
- Question #7: What do the Annunaki have to say about other galactic species, how many are they and how much interaction between species is going on here and elsewhere in the Milky Way galaxy and universe?
- Answer of the Anunnaki-Ulema
- Question #8: Is there a stargate in New York City?
- Answer of the Anunnaki-Ulema
- Question #9: How many stargates exist across the planet?
- Answer of the Anunnaki-Ulema
- Question #10: Are there specific times when they can be used or are they always open?
- Answer of the Anunnaki-Ulema
- Question #11: I heard one of the reasons for the illegal invasion of Iraq was to shut down their stargates and the U.S. military has built bases on top of them, as well as building bases over ancient archaeological sites of Anunnaki temples/ libraries/ abodes.)
- Question #12: Do the home planets of extraterrestrials visiting/ inhabiting earth exist in higher dimensions within our own galaxy?
- Answer of the Anunnaki-Ulema
- Question #13: What is the method of propulsion to travel interdimensionally and what do these ships look like and consist of?
- Answer of the Anunnaki-Ulema

- Question #14: What are Anunnaki ships made of and how do they look?
- Answer of the Anunnaki-Ulema
- Question #15: What are Anunnaki ships and extraterrestrial crafts made of and how do they look?
- Note
- Answer of the Anunnaki-Ulema

38. On activating the Conduit, decontaminating or cleansing ourselves, galactic species in the Milky Way, galaxy and universe, stargates, invasion of Iraq, Anunnaki and extraterrestrial spaceships and UFOs

Questions by A.M., New York.

Question #1: Are the Sumerian gods Enlil, Enki, Inanna and Marduk still alive and will they be returning to earth in 2022 or not? (A question I asked Zechariah Sitchin in person November 2007 but he did not answer)

Answer of Ulema Maximillien de Lafayette:

- 1. Enlil, Enki, Inanna and Marduk do not represent the whole hierarchy, and leadership of the Anunnaki. They are the Anunnaki Sinhars who landed on Earth, similar to other Anunnaki leaders who visited other worlds, galaxies, stars and planets.
- 2. The Anunnaki have visited 7 galaxies and interacted with hundreds upon hundreds of different and highly advanced extraterrestrial civilizations. They are all over the universe.
- 3. Millions of them traverse the universe and its multiple zones freely and regularly.
- 4. By life-span standards of the Anunnaki, Enlil, Enki, Inanna and Marduk are relatively young. For, Anunnaki have a very long longevity.
- 4. Some Anunnaki live 450,000 years, until the last cell or molecule in their mind and body deteriorates.
- 5. In some instances, the Anunnaki can self-reproduce themselves, and add more years to their longevity. So, the answer is yes, they are still alive.
- 5. Are they returning to Earth in 2022? According to Ulema Sadiq bin Bakri Al Ansari (512 year old and still alive), and honorable Master Li (217 year old and still alive), and as stated by Ulema Mordechai ben Zvi (270

year old and still alive), Sinhar Inannascharma and Sinhar Marduchk will lead the Anunnaki's return to Earth in 2022.
- 6. Their return to Earth has been already announced in the Anunnaki Matrix.
- 6. We also know where the Anunnaki shall land on planet Earth, and what assignments are already given to other leaders and commanders.
- 7. Some will be very peaceful, others alarming.

*** *** ***

Question #2: Is it possible for us earth humans to activate our Conduit ourselves here on earth, and if so what is the technique to do so.

Answer of Ulema Maximillien de Lafayette:

- 1. No, it is not possible.
- 2. You need to study with an Anunnaki-Ulema.
- 3. However, you can partially active one zone in your Araya through the "Transmission of the Mind" technique, and other techniques such as:
- a- The Abgaru introspection, if guided by an adept;
- b- The Anshekadoora-abra technique;
- c- The Afkir-r'-Tanawar, so on.

Note: These techniques, as well as other techniques and orientation training are fully discussed in de Lafayette's book "The Forbidden Book of Ramadosh." The Spanish edition book was translated by Laura Lebron.

*** *** ***

Question #3: When will Sinhar Marduchk's notes for 2022 be published?

Answer of the Anunnaki-Ulema:

- 1. Sinhar Ambar Anati has authorized the release of the "Mouza-Karaat of Sinhar Marduchk" (Notes/Diary of Sinhar Marduchk). It is our plan to publish the Mouza-Karaat before the last quarter of 2009.
- 2. The publication shall contain both the original notes as prescribed in Ana'kh (The Anunnaki's language), and the translation in English.
- 3. Some chapters shall contain transliteration as well.

*** *** ***

Question #4: What material /spiritual /lifestyle changes would we need to make in order to decontaminate or cleanse ourselves as much as possible prior to the return in 2022?

Note:
To answer to this question, would require pages upon pages, and intensive/extensive lists of prerequisites.
Ulema de Lafayette has already answered a major part of these questions in many of his books.

*** *** ***

Question #5: Is it possible that mind controlling frequencies can be remotely transmitted into our homes through devices such as the cable box or TV or other electronic instruments?
Steven Greer's book Hidden Truth, Forbidden Knowledge says yes.
Answer of the Anunnaki-Ulema:
- Absolutely. Dr. Greer told the truth.

Question #6: Have you read "Alien Interview"? In it the EBE says she is a member of the Domain Expeditionary Force sent from the Domain to explore, investigate and conquer this part of the galaxy en route to the galactic center, and claim the Domain to be an extremely old and very advanced civilization.

Answer of the Anunnaki-Ulema:
- 1. We do not read material and work written by humans.
- 2. However, we are fully aware that 99.99% of what has been written and said by Western authors and ufologists (Especially in the United States of America) about the Anunnaki, their history, other galactic civilizations, the origin of Man, alien technology, parallel dimensions, and non terrestrial spacecrafts were false, silly, and childish. Especially those so-called messages received from the stars, telepathic communications with extraterrestrials, and channeling with "Higher Beings".
- 3. The cosmic universe and its Two Wheels of Harmony do not function in this manner.
- 4. You have to understand (and get used to, and once for good and for ever), that extraterrestrials do not mingle with people in their homes, do not volunteer to provide galactic information, messages and instruction, do not telepathically communicate with individuals (Except in those rare cases of abductions by the Grays) to announce and/or to deliver any sort and any kind of revelations, messages, warnings, teachings, and instruction. They do NOT!
- 5. It is these sorts/kinds of claims, idiotic and childish statements, false reports, arrogant assumptions, bizarre theories about aliens and alien encounters, badmouthing few honest writers who touched the face of the truth but were ridiculed or maliciously attacked by ignorant and vindictive people, the totally untruthful and fabricated statements and accounts reported or given by so-called experiencers and messengers, the self-serving and egoistic ufologists, self-proclaimed researchers, so-called field investigators, the fraudulent mediums/contactors, twisted accounts from abductees and alleged contactees, the ridiculous channelers, and fake psychics that destroy the credibility of ufology! The world/field of ufology is

unhealthy! Ufology has become a religion; a dangerous cult!

*** *** ***

Question #7: What do the Annunaki have to say about other galactic species, how many are they and how much interaction between species is going on here and elsewhere in the Milky Way galaxy and universe?

Answer of Ulema Maximillien de Lafayette:

- 1. There are millions upon millions upon millions of all kinds, categories and levels of galactic civilizations in the universe.
- 2. And the universe encompasses so many layers of :

a- Existences,
b- Dimensions,
c- Spheres,
d- Zones,
e- Species,
f- Past worlds,
g- Present worlds,
h- Future worlds,
i- All kinds of space-time memories and projections,
j- Mind-matter-anti-matter manifestations,
k- Vibrational beings and life-forms,
l- Multidimensional beings and life-forms,
m- Intradimensional beings and life-forms,
n- Extraterrestrial beings and life-forms,
o- Intraterrestrial beings and life-forms,
p- Holographic entities, beings and life-forms.
It is a very very complex and complicated universe, and not always welcoming and peaceful.

*** *** ***

Question #8: Is there a stargate in New York City?
Answer of the Anunnaki-Ulema:
- Absolutely.

*** *** ***

Question #9: How many stargates exist across the planet?

Answer of Ulema Maximillien de Lafayette:

- 1. First, it is extremely important to understand or to try to understand the major characteristics, properties and enormous differences between:
- a- Gateway(s);
- b- Ba'ab(s);
- c- Time-pocket(s);
- d- Space pocket(s);
- e- Mad-khal(s);
- f- Mikh-Raaj(s);
- g- Stargate(s);
- h- Space diving lines;
- i- Time dividing lines;
- j- Intersections of multiple layers of the universe, etc...
- 2. Even though all of the above are separately grouped under "Stargates".

Note: (a) to (j) are discussed, and explained step-by-step, and at length in de Lafayette's book "The Anunnaki Ulema Final Warning: Humanity destiny, UFOs threat, and the extraterrestrials final solution.Revised"

- 2. There are 70 "Gateways-Stargates" across/around planet Earth.
- 3. Not all of them serve the same purpose.
- 4. Not all of them function, open and close in the very same manner.

*** *** ***

Question #10: Are there specific times when they can be used or are they always open?

Answer of Ulema Maximillien de Lafayette:
- 1. Stargates/Gateways/Ba'abs function, open, and close according to a Matrix that establishes:
- a- Specific times;
- b- Specific entrances and exists called respectively Mad-khal(s) and Mikh-Raaj(s);
- c- Mass, matter and anti-matter.
- 2. Stargates, Gateways, and Ba'abs are not always open, because a permanent "opening" will create cosmic catastrophes.
- 3. A permanent "opening" will suck up everything that exists in its perimeter, like the black holes.
- 4. A permanent or quasi-permanent "opening" will de-fragment, disintegrate, and annihilate molecules, space boundaries, particles, atoms, matter and mass, including dark energy, and "God Particle".
- 5. Should these de-fragmentations, disintegrations, and annihilations occur, the universe will cease to exist.

*** *** ***

Question #11: I heard one of the reasons for the illegal invasion of Iraq was to shut down their stargates and the U.S. military has built bases on top of them, as well as building bases over ancient archaeological sites of Anunnaki temples/ libraries/ abodes.)

Answer of the Anunnaki-Ulema:
- Nonsense!

*** *** ***

Question #12: Do the home planets of extraterrestrials visiting/ inhabiting earth exist in higher dimensions within our own galaxy?

Answer of the Anunnaki-Ulema:

- Yes and way beyond.

*** *** ***

Question #13: What is the method of propulsion to travel interdimensionally?

Question # 14: And what do these ships look like and consist of?

Author's note: Answers to these two questions were provided in several books I have written. It is even impossible to summarize herewith pertinent information and findings.
Besides, it will take so many pages in this book. Please email me and I will refer you to the books dealing with your questions.
Email: delafayette6@aol.com

*** *** ***

Question #15: What are Anunnaki ships and extraterrestrial crafts made of and how do they look?

Answer of the Anunnaki-Ulema:

- **1.** The UFOs and USOs are the spaceships of the Grays who live here on Earth and underwater.
- **2.** They are made from special metal and a blend of material/substances totally unknown to humans.
- **3.** They are "coated" with:
- a- Protection shields;
- b- Anti-matter frames;
- c- Invisibility belts;
- d- Anti-gravity circumferences;
- e- Anti-metal fatigue, and anti-erosion properties, thus allowing them to jump from time pocket to another time pocket, and from space pocket to another space pocket. These maneuvers explain their erratic, irregular "flying" (In fact, they do not fly, they jump) pattern and sharp and sudden angular turns and spiral acceleration.

- **4.** They come in all shapes and forms ranging from:
- a- Circular;
- b- Conical (Conic);
- c- Triangular;
- d- Crescent;
- e- Half crescent; and half crescent with an angular tail;
- f- Cigar shape;
- g- Spheroids, also called "Flattened Spheres";
- h- Rings;
- i- Balls of lights;
- j- Oval;
- k- Egg shape;
- l- Diamond shape;
- m- Lampshade shape;
- n- Cylindrical;
- o- Probes;
- p- Small carriers;
- **5.** Grays UFOs and USOs have a multitude of spectral colors and shades such as:
- a- Bluish in day time;
- b- Bluish-grayish in day time;
- c- Orange in day time;
- d- Reflective in day time;
- e- Shiny (Aluminum-Silver-Chrome colors);
- f- Luminous in the dark or night time;
- g- Extremely bright in the dark or night time;
- h- Different and constantly changing colors from burning magnesium to fluorescent blue-green, in the dark or night time;
- i- Sudden alteration/variation from greenish-blue to red-orange, with intense white-blue underside or under the "belly" of the craft, in the dark or night time;
- j- The total spectral colors (Range and intensity) range from silver to red, yellow, orange, green, violet and blue.
- **6-** They emit various gases, to name a few:
- Hydrogen;
- Acetylene;
- Translucent plasma;
- Helium;

- Oxygen;
- Carbon dioxide;
- Argon;
- Krypton, so on...
- 7- They produce several physical, mental, emotional, psychological, psycho-somatic and bio-organic effects on human beings, animals, and the environment, to name a few:
- a- An intense heat;
- b- Continuous increase of temperature;
- c- Radio active emission and rays;
- d- Paralysis;
- e- Immobilization;
- f- Vision impairment;
- g- Burning the skin;
- h- Laps of memory;
- i- Difficulty in breathing;
- j- Lost of consciousness;
- k- Electrical shocks;
- l- Cars engines stop to work;
- m- Vehicles motors misfire;
- n- Headlamps regularly went out;
- o- Emission of electromagnetic energy;
- p- Painful pricklings;
- q- Disruption of electrical circuits;
- r- Amnesia;
- s- Headache;
- t- Eye pains;
- u- Nausea; so on...
- **8.** The Anunnaki ships called Merkaba and Markaba are completely different from the UFOs and USOs you see in the skies.
- a- They are much much bigger;
- b- They are always accompanied by a mother-ship that stays around the orbit of the Earth;
- c- The mother-ship houses multiple and smaller crafts, usually stored in the lowest section (Belly) of the mother-ship;

- d- They produce a loud sound when they take off from a land-base;
- e- The spaceship top section has a dome made from translucent material, resembling a diamond ring;
- f- This upper section (At the very top) of the spaceship serve as a navigation and control command center;
- g- Below the crystal ring, there are four to five circular and parallel compartments connected to the main engine of the craft;
- h- I have used the word "Engine" for lack of proper terminology, because alien spaceships of any category do not have engines or motors, some time, the whole craft serves as a propulsion catalyst.
- i- The larger Anunnaki spaceships are noted for their arched back side.
- j- The lower part or level of the spaceship have circular rings rotating independently from each other; these rings when they start to spin, they produce the lift, activate the spiral (Oval or circular) propulsion system, and instantly neutralize gravity.
- k- To the human eyes, the rings appear like wide-spread wings and/or a helicopter blade;
- i- The central/lower wheel (the fifth one) spins at a great speed;
- j- All wheels spin independently from each other in different directions; there is no synchronization in their motion and circular rotation;
- k- From the lower part of the spaceship (Belly), extend four rectangular sections that change to oval shape, when the craft has reached an altitude of 200 feet;
- l- On take off, these four sections remain inside the body of the craft. But when the craft lands, they "emerge" from the body of the craft to provide support for landing, even though they never touch the ground;
- m- These four sections are sometime called the "Legs of the ship"' they are clearly visible to the naked eyes, because they look like long, extended and straight forks, brightly polished, of a golden or amber color that changes to highly polished brass color;
- n- Fraction of seconds, before the craft lands while still hovering in a semi-circular motion, the "legs" of the ship

begin to rotate on their own axis, and the very end or extremity of the legs become flat;
- o- The spaceship does not a cockpit or a flight deck for obvious reasons.
- p- The entrance gate or door of the ship is never visible at first sight. The gate or the door opens and closes in a revolving manner.
- q- Once, the door or the gate stops to rotate, a sort of an extended rail (consisting of several lined up rectangular sections attached to each other by very thin rows of tubes) extends from the lower body of the ship, and its extension suddenly widens, and opens up to reveal a circular entrance/exit.

Note: This was a very brief descriptive summary of the exterior of the craft. To learn more on the interior of the craft, the compartments of the pilots and passengers, the vault that contains the main apparatus, the navigation instruments, the prime operation room, the ammunitions and weapons system, etc., you have to read the scientific report on all types of Markaba. Again, you have dig out this report in various chapters of my previously published books.

*** *** ***

39. On sharing the same God with extraterrestrials, the great book of knowledge, end of our planet, the truth in the Bible, are the Anunnaki the bad guys?
⌘⌘⌘

- Question #1: Do we all share the same god?
- Answer of the Anunnaki-Ulema
- Question #2: Did they make us?
- Answer of the Anunnaki-Ulema
- Question #3: When will we know the full truth?
- Answer of the Anunnaki-Ulema
- Question #4: What is man here for?
- Answer of the Anunnaki-Ulema
- Question #5: Is there a great book of knowledge?
- Answer of the Anunnaki-Ulema
- Question #6: When will our planet end?
- Answer of the Anunnaki-Ulema
- Question #7: Is the Bible the truth?
- Answer of the Anunnaki-Ulema
- Question #8: Why don't they show them self to people who seek?
- Answer of the Anunnaki-Ulema
- Question #9: Will humans destroy earth?
- Answer of the Anunnaki-Ulema
- Question #10: The Anunnaki are the bad guys, don't you agree?
- Answer of the Ulema

39. On sharing the same God with extraterrestrials, the great book of knowledge, end of our planet, the truth in the Bible, are the Anunnaki the bad guys?

Note: Questions from Jamie Havican
Questions:

Question #1: Do we all share the same god?
Answer of the Anunnaki-Ulema:
- No.

*** *** ***

Question #2: Did they make us?
Answer of the Anunnaki-Ulema:
- Affirmative.

*** *** ***

Question #3: When will we know the full truth?
Answer of the Anunnaki-Ulema:
- Not before 2021 or 2022.

*** *** ***

Question #4: What is man here for?

Answer of the Anunnaki-Ulema:
- 1. The answer depends on your religious beliefs.
- 2. Your priest, pastor, rabbi, cheik and other religious dignitaries, figures and preachers have already handy and well-crafted answers.
- 3. But you got to remember that religions for centuries and centuries fought knowledge, science, astronomy,

physics, mathematics, cosmology, autopsy, medicine, jailed, exiled and killed scientists.
- 4. By the name of God, and faith, they burned hundreds of thousands of people in public places, mutilated their bodies in tortures donjons, and refused them burial rites.
- 5. The answer also depends on the person you are addressing the question.
- 6. Is she or is he a traditional scientist, an avant garde futurist, a physician, a cosmologist, an anthropologist, a psychologist, a metaphysic teacher, a qauntum physics professor, a raconteur, an elementary school teacher in Texas or Barbados, a spiritual medium, a psychic to the stars, a colorful channeler, a Biblical scholar, a mental case nerd posting hilarious stuff on the Internet, an expert in ancient languages? Or something else?
- 7. Theories and assumptions on the subject are endless!
- 8. To tell you the truth, only few people and beings of any dimension knew why you are here and where you are going, and where you will end up; here are some names:
- a- The Anunnaki because they have created you,
- b- The Igigi because they have witnessed your genetic creation in the Chimiti (Laboratories, tubes, containers) of the Anunnaki,
- c- Few other galactic races like the Lyrians, the Nordics, the Zeta Reticulians, because they have discussed your faculties, mental and bio-organic "properties", nature and especially your possible admittance into the Federation of Light and its Majliss (Council), following the initiative of the Anunnaki.
- d- The early Phoenician, Arwadian cosmologists, and the offspring of the Anunnaki, and few of their remnants.
- e- The Anunnaki-Ulema.

*** *** ***

Remember that other humans (More exactly quasi-humans and other semi intelligent life-forms) were already here on Earth, long before the Anunnaki and/or any other extraterrestrial races visited Earth, and the idea or concept of "God" were known to mankind.

Ulema de Lafayette said: Some were the product and results of:
- a- Photosynthesis,
- b- Metabolism,
- c- Bio-organic metamorphosis,
- d- Cosmic dust,
- e- Space particles,
- f- Galactic molecules,
- g- Space bubbles,
- h- Meteors containing blocks of life,
- i- Multiple universes collisions,
- j- Genetic manipulations,
- k- Several evolutionary processes, you name it.

Those people, entities and life-forms did not know where they were here, and why they were created; they did not even know on what dimension they lived. And even the Anunnaki themselves did not know what they were here on Earth, and what were the purposes and reasons for their existence.
But the Anunnaki know very well why the early prototypes of Bashars (Humans) and the final product of their experimental genetic manipulations that shaped up the final shape of modern humans were created, and what purposes they must verve.
They created you to as labor manpower, as a work force, as machines and robots to work the fields, to feed them, to serve them, etc.
All these ideas and reasons are documented in the poems, epics, and tales they left us, and which were recorded in the Akkadian/Sumerian clay tablets, and the cosmogony of the early Phoenicians.
But things became to change, when the Anunnaki started to show interest in the human race, and manifest affection toward your ancestors. Especially, when the early humans were allowed to mix with their women and men, and more precisely, when the Anunnaki began to marry Earth's women and father their children.
At that particular moment in history, the Anunnaki changed their plans for the human race, and improved their mental and physical faculties. Instead of the 13 primordial faculties they

"inserted" in their brains and bodies, The Anunnaki added more faculties and capabilities, such as writing poetry, composing music, erecting cities, mapping the skies, establishing rules for their communities, developing sophisticated irrigation systems, discovering mineralogy, etc.

And when the Anunnaki discovered (to their greatest delight and surprise) that humans after all are not so inferior and limited in their imagination, endurance and creativity, the Anunnaki decided on a new fate, a new destiny, and new role for humanity on the landscape of the universe, this dimension and the ones before:

The new fate, the destiny and the new role of humans beings can be summarized as follows:

- a-The Anunnaki will develop for the human beings, a gradual and systematic plan to reach the ultimate level of awareness, understanding of the universe, and living in absolute harmony and elegant synchronization with the cosmos;
- b-The Anunnaki will guide humanity toward the ultimate purpose and target of the creation, when they reach higher dimensions of existence: Perpetual happiness, peace, love, quasi-immortality, a state of mind free of illness, diseases, financial worries, aggression, wars, physical pain, ignorance, and above all the attainment of "Ra-hat Dae-mat", which means state of perfection and perpetual knowledge.

This is what is going to be the fate of all humans. They were not created and placed on Earth to accomplish and attain all these wonderful things, but finally, the Anunnaki decided to facilitate the process by which all humans can reach ultimate peace, knowledge and happiness.

Nobody else in the whole universe will stand by the human race to achieve this, except the Anunnaki.

The Anunnaki are humanity's only hope and salvation.

*** *** ***

Question #5: Is there a great book of knowledge?
Answer of the Anunnaki-Ulema:
- The Book of Ramadosh.

*** *** ***

Question #6: When will our planet end?
Answer of the Anunnaki-Ulema.
Ulema Oppenheimer said:
- 1. Soon or later, the world will come to an end.
- 2. The end of Earth is some 7.5 billion to 7.6 years from now.

*** *** ***

Question #7: Is the Bible the truth?

Answer of the Anunnaki-Ulema
Ulema Mordechai ben Zvi said:
- 1. Not everything in the Bible is factual.
- 2. Some passages are the product of a vivid imagination and very colorful fabrication, such as the Genesis, the story of the creation of Adam and Eve, the Exodus, the Ten Commandments; the story of Jericho; The story of Sodom and Gomorra, so on.
- 3. Generally speaking, the Bible is a beautiful piece of literature.

*** *** ***

Question #8: Why don't they show themselves to people who seek?

Answer of the Anunnaki-Ulema
Ulema Mordechai ben Zvi said:

- 1. They did! The two big questions remain: Who are the true seekers? Who are those who are entitled to?

- 2. They have revealed themselves to the Mounawariin (Enlightened ones), to the Taa-'hiriin (The Pure ones), and to the Anunnaki-Ulema.
- 3. It is not enough to seek. You have to be 100% pure in thoughts, feelings, intentions and deeds.
- 4. And your mind's Araya and Conduit must be fully activated.
- 5. Are the Mounawariin 100% pure? Yes, they are. And is it possible to reach perfection and ultimate purity on Earth and/or in other dimensions? Yes, it is possible. We are not talking here about physical purity and physical perfection, but about the mental/spiritual ones.
- 6. How could you reach these ultimate standards of perfection and purity?
- 7. The Anunnaki-Ulema have taught for centuries, and still teach relevant techniques and methods.

*** *** ***

Question #9: Will humans destroy earth?
Answer of the Anunnaki-Ulema
Ulema Oppenheimer said:
- No!

*** *** ***

Question #10: The Anunnaki are the bad guys. Don't you agree?
- Author's answer: Do you still think so? Read, and read, and read again this book, and you will change your mind. And if you are still unconvinced, read the "Book of Ramdosh".

*** *** ***

40. On the Bando Project, and the study of the anatomy of dead aliens' bodies, and extraterrestrial survivors
⌘⌘⌘

- 1. What was the purpose of the Bando Project?
- 2. Is this secret project still going on?
- 3. What were the findings and results of the project
- Author's note/answer
- Bando Project
- I. Definition and introduction
- II. Allegations
- III. Former double agent's claims
- (CIA, KGB, MI5, Moscow Academy of Medicine)
- V. The Russian newspaper/website Pravda article

40. On the Bando Project, and the study of the anatomy of dead aliens' bodies, and extraterrestrial survivors

Note: Questions sent by Emanuel Pravo, Milan, Italy.
Questions:
- 1. What was the purpose of the Bando Project?
- 2. Is this secret project still going on?
- 3. What were the findings and results of the project

Author's note: No need to ask the Anunnaki-Ulema, for I have addressed the issue in my previous books. Here are some brief excerpts:

Bando Project:
I. Definition and introduction
II. Allegations
III. Former double agent's claims
(CIA, KGB, MI5, Moscow Academy of Medicine)
V. The Russian newspaper/website Pravda article

I. Definition and introduction:
Project Bando was established in 1949, for the purpose of studying the anatomy of dead aliens' bodies, and extraterrestrial survivors who were found on the site of two alleged UFO's crashes in the United States. Allegedly, CIA's files show that Bando Project medically examined aliens, named in the CIA's report as EBE (Extraterrestrial Biological Entities).
The Project supplied the United States government with "essential medical and anatomic data on aliens, and provided some answers to the theory of evolution." The program was allegedly terminated in 1974.

II. Allegations:
Insiders claimed that Bando Project is an "on going process" under various names; one of them is called Project Nomad. An insider alleged that FBI director J. Edgar Hoover called the CIA

and wrote to them many times, asking for "copies of the report on the recovery of the aliens' bodies, and the medical report of the examinations of the EBEs."

The insider added, "The Director was so upset...he got nothing from them, then the CIA told the Director to make a call to Gen X., who was in charge of the project.
They gave him his name and telephone number. The CIA told the Director that they had no interest in all this. The Director called the base and he spoke to the general. I don't know what they talked about. Later on, we learned that the bodies of the aliens were in the Blue Room..."

III. Former double agent's claims:
(CIA, KGB, MI5, Moscow Academy of Medicine):
In 1978, a former double agent (Now in retirement in Budapest) said (In his own words): "The CIA people were working on the Bando Project, and did medical examination of the bodies of the dead aliens at Langley. I know that because the KGB infiltrated the CIA, and one of our agents (Meaning a Russian) knew all about it.
He reported to the KGB and to Moscow Academy of Medicine. Something else I can tell you, they made two films of the autopsy and another fake one. At the beginning we did not know which film was the real one.
The fake copy was well-done, professionally looking.
The Moscow Academy of Science got a copy of one of the films. Later, a colonel from the KGB sold a copy of the film to MI5 (UK's security intelligence agency) for $10,000. I know this happened, because I saw a slip deposit from Moscow Narodny Bank.

IV. The Russian newspaper Pravda account:
Ironically, perhaps coincidently, in 2004, the semi-official Russian Pravda newspaper published the following article (As is, unedited, and as it appeared in its English version.
Do you remember that 10 years ago the old black-and-white film about the postmortem examination of the alien in the USA in 1947 was broadcast all over the world?

Headline: CIA and KGB were fighting for alien's dead body.

Text: Americans did their best to persuade the world that the film was a forgery, but failed. The tape, the camera, the medical examiners' instruments – all this was authentic", says Boris Shurinov, Chairman of the Russian UFO Society.

He has been collecting the materials on UFOs for many years. To distract people from their film, Americans made another one – about the postmortem examination of the alien in the Soviet Union.
"The idea of the movie with James Bond as its main character was about "flying saucer's" crash in the USSR, and all the footage of the incident was allegedly banned from the public by KGB.
Then the brave Americans purchased this secret archive from the corrupted Russians to familiarize public with it", says Boris Shurinov. "According to the movie, the disc fell down near the city of Sverdlovsk in November, 1968. They found it in March, 1969, KGB people arrived, the spot was encircled".
"I conducted investigation and discovered that the movie was a forgery. I found out that the "secret filming of 1969 took place in 1998 in the base of Mosfilm company in the town of Alabino, Moscow region. "The flying saucer was made of foam plastic", says Mr. Shurinov."
I even discovered that the filming of the "alien dissection" took place in Moscow Academy of Medicine, and even found the desk the "alien" was put on.
After that, at many international conferences of UFOs, I denounced this forged movie and the key liar – US expert on UFOs Paul Stonehill. However, I was not successful, as they called me a KGB man and anti-Semite (as Mr. Stonehill is a Jew, and I was denouncing him)".
According to Boris Shurinov, "95 per cent of the stories on UFOs are lies, but there is a fraction of truth in them. Americans faced this problem in the mid-40s. In 1942, US President Roosevelt received a note about a sudden air-raid warning:

On February 25 many flying objects appeared in the sky over Los Angeles, air defense forces decided that these were Japanese aircrafts and started shooting at them, but missed all the targets.
In 1947, US press registered more than 850 cases of UFO observation mentioning.
Americans started accusing the Soviet Union of testing its new aircrafts over the US territory. Soviet Vice Consulate had to make

a statement that "the USSR respects the sovereignty of all the states, and no way it could use other countries' territory as a testing ground.
The Soviet Union has more than enough on its own territory for conducting scientific research". At some point, as the interest in UFOs was growing, UFO "experts" were inventing more and more stories, and it became hard to distinguish real stories from lies.

*** *** ***

41. On "Barage Europa" (Extraterrestrial tunnels/structures)
⌘⌘⌘

- Question: I heard once Mr. de Lafayette talking about Barage Europa. I missed the beginning of his speech. What did he mean by Barage, and is this Barage related to extraterrestrial structures on Europa near Jupiter?
- Ulema de Lafayette's answer

41. On "Barage Europa" (Extraterrestrial tunnels/structures)

Question: I heard once Mr. de Lafayette talking about Barage Europa. I missed the beginning of his speech. What did he mean by Barage, and is this Barage related to extraterrestrial structures on Europa near Jupiter?

Ulema de Lafayette's answer:
Barage Europa is a term used by Russian cosmonaut to refer to extraterrestrial tunnels and structures on other planets. Some "spiritualists" locate these tunnels under water in the Atlantic Ocean.
Rubén Sobrino, a noted ufologist and a member of SEIP, reported (as is, and unedited): "On January 16 of this year, almost all the newspapers in our country echoed the same remarkable news item from Moscow, carried by the prestigious EFE news agency. The agency in question disclosed certain controversial statements made by Russian astrophysicist Boris Rodionov to Moscow's Komsomolskaya Pravda, in which he claimed to have proof of the existence of "a highly developed extraterrestrial civilization on one of the satellites of the planet Jupiter.

The astrophysicist also claimed that the enigmatic "flying saucer" phenomenon which has stimulated popular imagination worldwide could well be "outriders for this civilization."
Wielding a vast amount of scientific data and photographs transmitted by NASA's "Galileo" probe, Rodionov, a professor of Microphysics and Cosmophysics of the State Institute of Physical Engineering, stated that Europa, smallest of Jupiter's four main satellites, "was inhabited by an ancient and technologically advanced civilization."
Through the use of a high-powered computer and sophisticated photographic analysis technology, the scientist managed to obtain a close-up with a record-breaking resolution of nine kilometers from the satellite's surface, enabling him to make out the contours of what he calls pipes, tunnels and spherical domes.

The photo clearly shows--according to Rodionov--that the lines formerly considered as mere fissures by the scientific community actually cross over each other like a knot of expressways.

According to Rodionov, the variety of "pipelines" and "tunnels", having a diameter similar to the Channel that crosses the English Channel, is surprising. "There are 100 kilometer segments, as well as other pipelines having immense junctures or orifices between them."

Anyone may join the controversy, since the image in which Rodionov claims to see the aforementioned pipelines and tunnels is available to anyone having Internet access and a simple photo retouching program capable of analyzing it.

The photo, which is available from the NASA/JPL net server that provides images for the "Galileo" mission, in fact portrays a number of lines (fissures, in fact) which cross each other but never at different elevations, as the scientist has claimed.

Having a width of approximately 20 to 40 kilometers, and thousands of kilometers in length, it is believed that the fissures are attributable to a period of global expansion on Europa, caused by volcanic eruptions or geysers under its frosty surface, creating a series of fractures on the ice crust.

This news item would not go beyond being an amusing anecdote, were it not for the fact that it is the first time that a person related to the armed forces or the Russian Space Agency made similar statements to the press."

*** *** ***

42. On Bariya, and the Anunnaki's creation of Man
⌘ ⌘ ⌘

- Question #1: I can't read the Sumerian texts to understand what is going on. Primarily, I am interested in finding anything that tells me something about how the Anunnaki created us?
- Question #2: Where are those texts?
- Question #3: And something else, and without any offense to you, please guide me to authors other than the Ulema and your group who have found anything on this
- Question #4: And by the way, what did you mean by Bariya? I read about it in one of your books, and could not understand a thing."
- Authors' answers and comments by other scholars
- Bariya "Ba-riya'ah"
- I. Definition
- II. Bariya (The Creation) as described in the Sumerian texts
- III. The creation of humans
- Here are additional Akkadian/Sumerian clay tablets passages on the creation of the Man and pertinent comments by scholars, historians, linguists and the authors
- Ninlil, the legendary Sumerian "Queen Breeze"
- Marduk was the son of Ea
- In the Akkadian/Sumerian epic Enuma Elish, we read
- Inanna was the legendary Sumerian goddess who created the first 7 prototypes of mankind

- The Sumerian-Anunnaki goddess Nammu "Namma" and her son Enki created multiple forms of humans
- Ea killed Kingu, the demon son of Tiamat, and used his blood to create mankind
- Apsu and the creation of man
- From the Sixth Tablet
- From the Seventh Tablet

42. On Bariya, and the Anunnaki's creation of Man

Note: Questions sent by H. Petraki, Athens, Greece.
Question #1: I can't read the Sumerian texts to understand what is going on. Primarily, I am interested in finding anything that tells me something about how the Anunnaki created us?

Question #2: Where are those texts?

Question #3: And something else, and without any offense to you, please guide me to authors other than the Ulema and your group who have found anything on this.

Question #4: And by the way, what did you mean by Bariya? I read about it in one of your books, and could not understand a thing."

**Authors' answers and comments by other scholars:
Bariya "Ba-riya'ah"**
Ana'kh. Noun.
I. Definition
II. Bariya (The Creation) as described in the Sumerian texts
III. The Creation of humans

I. Definition:
Bariya is a term for the Creation in the Anunnaki's language.

II. Bariya (The Creation) as described in the Sumerian texts.
From Bariya, derived the primitive Arabic words Bari (Creator; God), and Baria (Creation; creatures.)
The Sumerian Creation:
Only one account of the Sumerian Creation has survived, but it is a suggestive one. This account functions as an introduction to the story of "The Huluppu-Tree":
"In the first days when everything needed was brought into being,

In the first days when everything needed was properly nourished,
When bread was baked in the shrines of the land,
And bread was tasted in the homes of the land,
When heaven had moved away from the earth,
And earth had separated from heaven,
And the name of man was fixed;
When the Sky God, An, had carried off the heavens,
And the Air God, Enlil, had carried off the earth."-Sumerian text.

III. The Creation of humans:

The Anunnaki god said:
"Mix the heart of the clay that is over the abyss,
The good and princely fashioners will thicken the clay,
You, Nammu do you bring the limbs into existence;
Ninmah earth-mother or birth goddess will work above you,
The goddesses of birth will stand by you at your fashioning;
O my mother, decree its [the newborn's fate,
Ninmah will bind upon it the imageof the gods,
It is man..." Translated by Jacobsen

*** *** ***

Here are additional Akkadian/Sumerian clay tablets passages on the creation of the Man and pertinent comments by scholars, historians, linguists and the authors:

The Sumerian texts include various versions of the creation of mankind by a multitude of Anunnaki's gods and goddesses. Some passages in the Sumerian texts refer to different creators, as well as to multiple genetic experiments.
There is no reference to one singular genetic creation of the early human races, or a solid certainty to the fact that mankind was genetically created by one single god. In fact, a multitude of gods and goddesses created different types and categories of human beings, to name a few:

1-Ninlil, the legendary Sumerian "Queen Breeze", was also called Aruru, Ninhursag, Ninhursanga, the Lady of The Mountains, the ruler of the heavens, underworld, wind, earth, and grain, wife of Enlil and the mother of Nanna/Utu experimented with different forms and shapes of early human beings.
Ninlil also created Endiku.
In the Epic of Gilgamesh we read:
"...she created mankind...so numerous...
she thrust her hands into the waters
and pinched off some clay, which she dropped in the wilderness,
in the wilderness she made Endiku the hero..."
And in another passage, it was written:
"My friend Endiku whom I loved has turned to clay...died,
returned to the clay that formed him..."

2-Marduk was the son of Ea and husband of Sarpanitu, the sun-god, and also the god of war, fire, earth and heaven, and one of the major creators of heroes, gods and humans. He waged a ravaging war against Tiamat, dismembered her, and used several parts of her body to create the world and the early races of humanity.

In the Akkadian/Sumerian epic Enuma Elish, we read:
"He opened his mouth
and unto Ea he spake
That which he had conceived
in his heart he imparted unto him
My blood will I take
and bone will I fashion
I will make man, that man may
I will create man who shall inhabit the earth,
That the service of the gods
may be established,
and that their shrines may be built..."

3-Inanna was the legendary Sumerian goddess who created the first 7 prototypes of mankind.
Many other civilizations worshipped her under different names, such as Astarte, Istar, Ashtar, Asherat.

Inanna was called Ashtaroot and Ishtar in Phoenician; Ashtoreth and Ashtaroth in Hebrew; Ashteroth in Canaanite; Atargatis in Greek.

4-The Sumerian-Anunnaki goddess Nammu "Namma" and her son Enki created multiple forms of humans, sometimes using clay, and some other times blood of warriors they slaughtered.

5-Ea killed Kingu, the demon son of Tiamat, and used his blood to create mankind. Ea was the son of Anu. Sometimes he is mentioned as the son of Anshar.
Ea created Zaltu as a complement to Ishtar.

6-Apsu and the creation of man:
Sumerian/Akkadian/Mesopotamian. Noun. A primeval

From the clay of Apsu man was fashioned.
According to the Akkadian/Sumerian clay tablets found in Iraq, Apsu advised mankind when the gods of heavens and Earth decided on harming the human race. Apsu granted Adapa , wisdom, understanding and knowledge, and sent him to teach mankind.

7-From the Sixth Tablet:

We selected these passages:
"23. "It was Kingu who created the strife,
24. "Who made Tiamat to revolt, to join battle with thee."
25. They bound him in fetters they brought him before Ea, they inflicted punishment on him, they let his blood,
26. From his blood he (i.e., Ea) fashioned mankind for the
service of the gods, and he set the gods free.
27. After Ea had fashioned man he ... laid service upon him.

8-From the Seventh Tablet:
I selected these passages:

26. Lord of the holy incantation, who maketh the dead to live,
27. He felt compassion for the gods who were in captivity.
28. He riveted on the gods his enemies the yoke which had been resting on them.

29. In mercy towards them he created mankind,
30. The merciful one in whose power it is to give life.
31. His words shall endure for ever, they shall never be forgotten,
32. In the mouth of the black-headed* whom his hands have made.

*Note: Here the title "Black-headed" refers to all mankind, but it is sometimes used by the scribes to distinguish the population of the Euphrates Valley from foreign peoples of light complexions.

***   ***   ***

43. On Mu, Anunnaki's interference in Earth's affairs, the reptilians, departure and return of the Anunnaki, God, religions, and life after death
⌘ ⌘ ⌘

- Question #1: MU's connection with the Anunnaki. What can you tell me about the lost continent of MU?
- Answer of the Anunnaki-Ulema
- Question #2: Where are the Anunnaki right now and why don't they interfere on our planet anymore?
- Answer of the Anunnaki-Ulema
- Question #3: We see, nearly every ancient civilization somehow had some sort of contact with the Anunnaki. So what did happen after that? Where did Anunnaki go and why?
- Answer of the Anunnaki-Ulema
- Question #4: Is it true that lots of Earth governments including US are controlled or ruled by an Alien race called reptilians?
- Answer of the Anunnaki-Ulema
- Question #5: So, if modern religions are false, is there a God Almighty?
- Note
- Question #6: What does happen to us when we die?
- Author's note
- Question #7: Were the prophets controlled by Anunnaki or they have manipulated the people as they wished?
- Answer of the Anunnaki-Ulema

- Question #8: Do you know anything about old Turks named Gokturks?
- Answer of the Anunnaki-Ulema
- Question #9: Do you have any knowledge about Turks and their connection with Anunnaki or Sirius system?
- Answer of the Anunnaki-Ulema
- Question #10: In the Lost book of Enki, Zecharia Sitchin wrote, the mysterious face on Mars (which is still unaccepted by NASA) was Anunnaki Alalu's graveyard. Do you know is it true?
- Answer of the Anunnaki-Ulema
- Question #11: Are Enlil, Enki, Anu etc. still alive?
- Answer of the Anunnaki-Ulema
- Note
- Question #12: Can you write some info about you? Where and when did you born, how did you go and learn the ways of the Ulema , etc.?
- Answer of the authors

43. On Mu, Anunnaki's interference in Earth's affairs, the reptilians, departure and return of the Anunnaki, God, religions, and life after death

Questions asked by Ismail Kemal Ciftcioglu, Turkey. (Unedited, and as received):

Question #1: This is the most important question for me. In any of the books I read, I haven't come to an information about lost continent of MU's connection with the Anunnaki. I assume you know lots of things about it.
According to James Churchward's books, MU was even older than Atlantis and home of the human civilization. Humans migrated from MU to all over the world. But we know that Anunnaki were in Mesopotamia. So what about it? What can you tell me about the lost continent of MU?

Answer of the Anunnaki-Ulema:
According to the legend and esoteric myths, Mu was a large continent of an advanced civilization. It sunk in the ocean many thousands of years ago. The story or Myth of Mu appeared for the first time in the 19th century, thanks to the writings of Augustus Le Plongeon (1825-1908), who claimed that the survivors of Mu went to the Americas and established the Mayan Empire.
Then, in the first half of the 20th century, the prolific writer and visionary extraordinaire James Churchward popularized the story of Mu in a series of books he wrote: "The Children of Mu" published in 1931; "The Lost Continent of Mu" published in 1933, and "The Sacred Symbols of Mu", published in 1935. And in the 1930's, Kamal Atatürk (Baba Kamal) then leader of Turkey, your majestic country, generously funded an academic and scientific research on Mu.
The great Turkish leader thought, that maybe, he will be able to establish a direct link or some sort of connection betweek Turkey and the word's first civilizations that could include the Aztec, and the Maya. Unfortunately, all attempts to prove the existence of MU failed.

However, Ulema Sharif Al Takki Al Zubyani (1797-1877) stated that Mu did exist some 50,000 years ago. He added that the original name of Mu was Mari, and it was inhabited by people who were very advanced in "Ilm Al Falak", meaning space science. An enormous explosion happened on the continent, caused by the reflections of lights and rays emitted by gigantic "Miraya", which means mirrors.

Coincidentally or strangely enough, the Anunnaki and Ulemite literature referred to Miraya as a galactic tool used to receive and emit cosmic messages, a sort of beam (Possibly atomic or laser), as well as to record and decode events from the past, the present and the future. Al Zubyani added: "Those mirrors were also used as weapons, and if they are not handled properly, they could destroy a whole country."
Those who know Arabic, including the archaic dialect of the Arab Peninsula, and Ana'kh will find out that there is a very close relation (Perhaps linguistically only) between the Name Mari and the Arabic, pre-Islamic word Mir'aat (Mir'-aat and Miraya) which means in both languages (Ana'kh and Arabic) mirror.
Strangely enough, the French word "Miroir" and the English word mirror derive directly from the Ana'kh (Anunnaki language) Miraya.
So here we have a million year old Anunnaki word "Miraya", a 50,000 year old name "Mari", a 7,000 year old Ulemite word "Mirra-ya", and a 5,000 year old Arabic word Miraya! Any connection?

*** *** ***

Question #2: Where are the Anunnaki right now and why don't they interfere on our planet anymore?

Answer of the Anunnaki-Ulema:

- 1. The Anunnaki are on their magnificent planet Ne.be.ru (Nibiru; Ashatari).
- They no longer interfere in humans' affairs for many reasons, to name a few:
- a. They are not interested in the human race, as they used to do thousands of years go, however, there are new serious concerns that made them monitor Earth and the human beings at distance.
- b. Earth is no longer one of their kingdoms (Or colonies);
- c. Earth does not meet their needs, supply them with what they need, or provide them with any significant resource(s);
- d. The Anunnaki do not need humans for any reason;
- e. The Anunnaki do no longer need the human beings as a labor force.
- f. The Anunnaki have finished their job on Earth.
- e. Grosso modo, neither Earth, nor the human beings are essential, meaningful or important to them, because you the human race and your planet Earth can offer nothing to the Anunnaki, at any level, whether it is culturally, scientifically, technologically, genetically, philosophically or galactically.

However, you have to keep in mind, that the Anunnaki are now very concerned about humans' DNA contamination, and the operations of the Grays on Earth.
These basically are the two principal reasons, why the Anunnaki are going to interfere in humans' affairs and Earth's condition, not now, but in the very near future. 2022 is the year and the time of the return of the Anunnaki to Earth. And you are going to have plenty of interferences from them.

*** *** ***

Question #3: We see, nearly every ancient civilization somehow had some sort of contact with the Anunnaki.
So what did happen after that?
Where did Anunnaki go and why?

Answer of the Anunnaki-Ulema:
- Already answered in our answer to your question #2.

*** *** ***

Question #4: Is it true that lots of Earth governments including US are controlled or ruled by an Alien race called reptilians?

Answer of the Anunnaki-Ulema:
- Nonsense!

*** *** ***

Question #5: So, if modern religions are false, is there a God Almighty?
Note: This question has been already answered in this book, please refer to the Table of Contents.

*** *** ***

Question #6: What does happen to us when we die?
Author's note: This question has been already answered in this book, please refer to the Table of Contents.

*** *** ***

Question #7: Were the prophets controlled by Anunnaki or they have manipulated the people as they wished?

Answer of the Anunnaki-Ulema:
- 1. The Anunnaki never controlled any prophet.
- 2. They have no reason to.

- 3. Prophets and organized religions do control people; this is exactly how they operate, and how they managed to stay in business, and became extremely influential.

*** *** ***

Question #8: Do you know anything about old Turks named Gokturks?

Answer of the Anunnaki-Ulema:
It is very important to learn and to remember that pre-historic Turkey as one of the strongholds and colonies of the Anunnaki. The early Hittites who lived in Turkey, and who have estalished one of the most formidable kingdoms on Earth had a close relation with the second expedition of the Anunnaki to planet Earth.
The very ancient Turkish word Göktürk mean "Heavenly Turks". Surrounding countries, and particularyly the Chinese in years to come called them "The Blue Princes", "The Blue Turks", and the "Celestial Blue People". It was told by Ulema Seif El Dinn Shawkat, that the Göktürk have inherited Ana'kh manuscripts given to them by the Arwadians.
The early Arwadians are acknowledged by the Anunnaki-Ulema to be the direct descendants of the Anunnaki. Here once again, we find a link between the ancient inhabitants of Turkey and the remnants of the Anunnaki.

*** *** ***

Question #9: Do you have any knowledge about Turks and their connection with Anunnaki or Sirius system?

Answer of the Anunnaki-Ulema:
A large segment of the population of your ancestors, the Hittites and their early leaders were Anunnaki's offspring and remnants in Anatolia (Asia Minor).

*** *** ***

Question #10: In the Lost book of Enki, Zecharia Sitchin wrote, the mysterious face on Mars (which is still unaccepted by NASA) was Anunnaki Alalu's graveyard. Do you know is it true?

Answer of the Anunnaki-Ulema:
- There are no frontiers to the imagination of Man!

*** *** ***

Question #11: Are Enlil, Enki, Anu etc. still alive?
Answer of the authors:
Author's note: This question has been already answered in this book, please refer to the Table of Contents.

*** *** ***

Question #12: Can you write some info about you? Where and when did you born, how did you go and learn the ways of the Ulema , etc.?

Answer of the authors:
- Read the book "On the Road to Ultimate Knowledge" co-authored byUlema Maximillien de Lafayette and Dr. Ilil Arbel.

*** *** ***

44. On teleportation (Barka-kirama)
⌘ ⌘ ⌘

- Question #1: What is the technique called Barka-kirama, Anunnaki-Ulema use for teleportation?
- Question #2: Please define Barka-kirama
- Note:
- I. Definition
- II. In ancient Middle Eastern literature
- III. The concept
- IV. The Tay Al Ard, self-teleportation and concept of the Alkiramat "Keramat"

44. On teleportation (Barka-kirama)

Questions:

Question #1: What is the technique called Barka-kirama, Anunnaki-Ulema use for teleportation?

Question #2: Please define Barka-kirama.

Authors' note: The following essay should answer your questions. It is taken from de Lafayette original work "Book of Ramadosh".

Barka-kirama:
Ana'kh. An Anunnaki extraterrestrial expression.
I. Definition
II. In ancient Middle Eastern literature
III. The concept
IV. The Taj Baba's theory
V. Tay Al Ard, self-teleportation and Alkiramat "Keramat"

I. Definition:
A blessing or an enlightenment (Tanwir) technique that develops teleportation.

It is composed of two words:
- **a**-Barka, which means blessing.
- **b**-Kirama, which means good deeds.

II. In ancient Middle Eastern literature:
Barka-kirama is a very important and a primordial Anunnaki's expression, because it is closely and directly related to Tay Al Ard, and Tay Al Makan, which mean teleportation. Tay Al Ard is an Ulemite/Arabic word. It is a metaphysical experience that produces a teleportation phenomenon; a secret esoteric practice of the Ulema and Allamah.

From Barka, derived:
- **a**-The Hebrew words Barak and Baraka (Blessings).
- **b**-The Arabic Baraka and Brakaat (Blessings).

From Kirama, derived:
- **a**-The Persian Keramat (Good deeds).
- **b**-The Arabic Kiramat (Honorable deeds).

III. The concept:
At one time, Barka-kirama, Tay Al Ard, and Tay Al Makan, were an arcane mixture of elements and esoteric substances used by Quelthulian ritualists in their teleportation experiences and experiments.

The Ulema claim that they have learned its secret and how its works from the Rou-hi-yin who are supreme beings from the Fifth dimension.

When Islam became a major religion in the Near East, and the Middle East, Tay Al Ard was banned by Prophet Muhammad, who called its practitioners "Min Ahl Al Nar", meaning verbatim: Those who are from fire.

Fire meant hell, or the kingdom of Al Shaytan (Satan, the devil). The Arabic pre-Islamic word Ulema was replaced by the Arabic Islamic word Allamah or Al Hallama. However, the Ulema and the Allamah were very different from each other in many ways.

The Ulema remained the custodians of the Anunnaki's secret knowledge and esoteric powers, while the Allamah were considered as the "Alamin", the learned ones and leading figures of letters, literature, science and religion.

Nevertheless, many Muslim teachers and spiritualists remain Ulema at heart. Many of them - secretly of course - joined the circle of the non-Muslim Ulema to learn the ultimate knowledge acquired from non-terrestrial beings. The Suphists were the first to join the Non-Muslim Ulema. Worth mentioning, that around, 850 A.D., Ulema and Allamah were semantically overlapping each other. And both words came to mean or express the same thing in the eye of Arab scholars, and in the Islamic world. Many Soufiyyin (Sufis) by joining the Ulema, learned some of the secrets of TayAl-Ard. They called it: "Tay Al Makan", meaning the folding of space.

It is composed of two Arabic words:

- **a**-Tay, which means folding or to fold.
- **b**-Al Makan, which means the Space; the location; the place.)

The Sufis replaced the word Al Makan with the word Al Ard.
The general meaning of Tay Al Ard or Tay Al Makan is to traverse the earth without moving. Al Munawarin claim that instead of physically moving from one place to another, an enlightened person can bring to himself, to where he is standing, the place he wanted to reach.

In other words, the earth of the place to reach has been displaced under the enlightened one's feet. Ironically, this pre-Islamic concept is now fully accepted by Muslim clerks, Cheiks and teachers of the Islamic Shari'a and Fuk'h, grouped together under the umbrella of Al Allamah.
Ulema or Allamah Qadhi, previously one of the leading figures of Allameh Tabatabaei explained Tay Al Ard as the termination of matter itself in the original location, and its re-appearance, manifestation, and re-creation in its final location, the place one wished to reach.
The Iranian Dehkhoda dictionary defined Tay Al Ard as: "An aspect of Keramat "Kiramat" (Extraordinary deeds of saints and holy people) in which instead of going toward a destination by taking a step forward, the earth turns itself toward the traverser rapidly, in a blink of an eye, regardless of how far the destination is." Ulema Ibn Al Nadim bin Ishaq al-Nadim (a.k.a. Al Warrak died on September 17, 995. He wrote the Kitab al-Fihrist.) explained this phenomenon by citing verses from the Quran, taken from Chapter Al Naml;
Verse: 27:38: Solomon said to his men: "O Chiefs, which of you can bring me the throne of Queen of Sheba before she and her envoys come to me in submission?"
Verse 27: 39: "Said an 'Ifrit of Al Jinns: "I will bring it to thee before thou rise from thy council. In fact, I have full power for this purpose, and may be trusted."
Verse 27:40: "Said one who had knowledge of the Book: "I will bring it to thee within a blink of any eye!" Then when the sage Solomon saw it placed right before him, he said: "This was done by the authority of God all mighty, my Lord."

Some Middle Eastern sages and teachers of religious esoteric dogmas suggested that according to these verses, the Ulema Asif ibn Al Birkhia teleported the throne of Queen of Sheba almost instantaneously, in a blink of an eye.
This was confirmed in a Hadith (Dialogue, a chat, or a discourse) by Jaafar Al Sadiq.
Allamah have explained this teleportation phenomenon very differently. They claimed that the teleportation occurred because Ulema Asif ibn Birkhia used one of the secret "Asma Al Allah Al Sab'a Al Husma." (One of the seven secret names of God.)
The knowledge and use of one of the secret holy and lovely names of God allowed Ulema Asif ibn Birkhia to teleport the throne.

The Ulema, students of the Anunnaki, briefly explained this phenomenon. Ulema Cheik Al Kabir said (Verbatim): "Time is represented with 2 lines not perfectly aligned; one for you, the other for what is not you.
Space is represented with two circles; one for you, the other for what is not you. If you manage to place yourself between one of the two lines and one of the two circles without touching the other line and the other circle, you will conquer time-space." The Taj Baba explains Tay Al Ard as the elapse of time and distances in the vicinity, and to reach far distant places in a flick of an eye.

It also means the transport for others to get there, and to call far distant things to become close at hands through the Karamat. It is a tradition and ritual practice related to Aulia Allah (Friends and favourites of God) that allow them to reach any place in the world instantly. The distance-time and places are wrapped up in a flick of second, and cross all that at once.

IV. The Tay Al Ard, self-teleportation and concept of the Alkiramat "Keramat":
Alkiramat "Keramat" is a Farsi (Iranian) and Arabic term meaning holy deeds that allow teleportation. Literally (Folding up of the earth) is the name for thaumaturgical teleportation in the mystical aspect of Islamic religious, esoteric, metaphysical and philosophical traditions.

In 2004, in a report to the United States Air Force (Dubbed: AFRL-PR-ED-TR-2003-0034), Dr. Eric W. Davis recommended the study of teleportation, which he defined as "The conveyance of persons or inanimate objects by psychic means."
Being an allegedly esoteric knowledge by nature, it is not known exactly how it takes place, but theories and explanations abound. The most prevalent theory has to do with the concept of consciousness and will. The person wishes to be some place, and he is then simply there an instant later.
This view can perhaps be understood from the perspective of Western philosophical idealism, where esse est percipi: If space does not have an objective reality, and reality itself is thought of as observer-based and a subjective entity, then ideas such as moving in space without actually physically moving are no longer unchartered possibilities.

In addition, the jinn are believed to possess this knowledge of transportation, however in a limited amount, according to the Allamah. Famous Sheikhs, Imams, and prominent figures such as Abusaeid Abolkheir or Rumi or Ak-Khidr, were believed to possess kiramat, and writings from medieval Islam are full of stories and reports of certain individuals possessing such a trait. For example, Idries Shah and Robert Graves mention the case where senior members of the Azimia order were reputed to appear, like many of the ancient Sheikhs at different places at one and the same time. Many other examples can be found in Attar's Tadhkirat Al-Awliya (Biographies of the Saints) or the works of Ibn Arabi, as well as other similar chronicles.
However, no one for sure has known the number and identity of all those who possess such knowledge, since according to Hujviri, those who hold such knowledge "do not know one another, and are not aware of the other's state of excellence, and are hidden from themselves and from mankind."
One of the most discussed phenomena of this supposedly esoteric knowledge is the event of traveling without actually moving. Islamic texts and records from the mystics are full of such accounts from various eras.
For example, Bayazid Bastami has many such accounts, colored with mystical flavors, surrounding his life.

In one account, he was asked, "They say you walk on water?"
"A piece of wood can do that too," he replied.

"They say you travel to Mecca at night and return by dawn?" he was asked.
"But a bird at flight can do that too" was his answer.
"So what is the meaning of being human?" he was asked.
"A human is he who does not fasten his heart to anything but God," he replied.

*** *** ***

45. On the various aliens capabilities of learning many languages and ways of using their methods to learn these languages
⌘⌘⌘

- Question # 1: How do all the various aliens know so many of our languages?
- Ulema Maximillien de Lafayette's answer
- Question # 2: Is there a way for us to learn using their methods?
- Authors' answer
- Question# 3: It would make the world a much better place if everyone could understand each other
- Answer

*** *** ***

45. On the various aliens capabilities of learning many languages and ways of using their methods to learn these languages

Note: Questions from Katy Fish, New York, and Wisconsin, USA.
Question# 1: How do all the various aliens know so many of our languages?

Ulema Maximillien de Lafayette's answer:
The Ana'kh was the Anunnaki's language on Earth for thousands of years. The early Mesopotamians, Phoenicians, inhabitants of Arwad, Ugarit, Amrit, Atlanteans, Hittites (Ancestors of the Turks), the early Hyskos (Ancestors of the Armenians), spoke Ana'kh.
In ancient and modern languages, in Eastern as well as in Western languages, you would find more than 7,000 Anunnaki's (Ana'kh) words, sometimes, Anunnaki's expressions and paraboles.
Thus, all our languages originated from the Anunnaki's language. This, should explain in part, why the "Aliens, as you called them" are familiar with "so many of our languages."

The Anunnaki's language (Ana'kh) had a major linguistic and epistemological influence on the languages of the ancient world, as well as upon the civilization, culture and religions of the ancient Near and Middle East, including but not limited to the Phoenicians, Sumerians, Assyrians, Akkadians, Babylonians, Mesopotamians, Copts, Hittites, Egyptians, Arabs, and Hebrews. Many of the Ana'kh words entered the early languages of those civilizations, and from the original Ana'kh, derived thousands of ancient Semitic and non-Semitic words and expressions, some very noticeable in Akkadian-Sumerian epics such as the Epic of Gilgamesh, and Enuma Elish, as well as in the Epic of the Phoenician Cosmogony.

For instance:
- 1-The Ana'kh word **Ab,** meaning father became Ab in Arabic, Abu and Abuya in Aramaic, Abba in Hittite, so on.

- 2-The Ana'kh word **Agirim,** means first baked clay.

Composed of two words:
- **a**-A, which means first,
- **b**-Girim, which means clay.

From Agirim, derived the Sumerian, Babylonian, and Akkadian word Girim (Clay).

*** *** ***

- 3-The Ana'kh word **A-kel** means food.

From A-kel, derived the Sumerian Akalum, and the Arabic Akel, which mean food.

*** *** ***

- 4-The Ana'kh word **Amamu**, means a front.

From Amamu, derived the Arabic word Amam, which means ahead; in front, and the Akkadian/Sumerian word Elamu, which means front.

*** *** ***

- 5-The Ana'kh word **Amram,** means good subjects of the Anunnaki's leaders; good union; highly developed communities.

Composed of two words:
- **a**-Am (Good; kind.)
- **b**-Ram (People; community; population; tribe.)

In Biblical studies, Amram means high people; kindred of the High; friend of Jehovah.

In primitive Arabic, Ram meant: People; group. Henceforth, the name of the Palestinian city Ramallah could be interpreted as the people of God, since Allah means to the Arabs and Muslims, what exactly the word Jehovah means to the Jews: God.

When Enki or Ea called upon Avraham, he told him: I am your god, and I am now changing your name from Av-raham to Ab-Raham, because you are going to lead my people as the father of my people on earth. Av became Ab. And Ab in all the 14 different

ancient languages of the Near East and the Middle East means father.
From the Ana'kh Ab, derived the words: Ab, Abu, Abi, Aba, Abba, Abuya, Abouna; all meaning the very same thing: Father. And from the Ana'kh word ram, derived the ancient Hebrew, Aramaic and Arabic word Ram: People.

Centuries later, Ram acquired a multitude of meanings.
For instance:
- **a**-In ancient Hebrew, Ram is pleasing.
- **b**-In Sanskrit mythology, Ram means supreme.
- **c**-In the pre-Islamic Arabic era, called Al-Gahiliya "Jahiliya" (Years of darkness), Ram meant a group of people. Synonym: Ra'bh.

From the Ana'kh Ram, we have today, the Arabic Ramy and the Spanish Ramos. In ancient times, the early Armenians called themselves the people of Ram. "They recognized themselves as the People of the Ram and their supreme deity was Khal-di. Thus was derived the land of the original Khaldini, later corrupted by Greeks in the times of Achaemenian to Chaldea, as mentioned in The Ark of Noah, David Fasold.

*** *** ***

- 6-The Ana'kh word **Aneshtu:** Knowledge; alert mind.

From Aneshtu, derived the Chaldean, Akkadian and Sumerian verb Neshtug (To understand).

*** *** ***

- 7- The Ana'kh word **Anganzir:** First Night; first darkness.

Composed from two words:
- **a**-An, which means first; the one.
- **b**-Ganzir, which means darkness.

From Aganzir, derived the Sumerian words Agenzer (Darkness) and Ganzir (The world of the dead.)

*** *** ***

- 9-The Ana'kh word **Annas-shim**, means group of passengers; group of people. From Annas, derived the Phoenician word Anat, which means people, and the proto-Arabic word Annas or An-naas, which means people; humans; groups gathering. It is still in use in contemporary Arabic.

    *** *** ***

- 10-The Ana'kh word **Aruru**, means creative force; the creator of life. From Aruru derived the Arabic word Rouh, and the Aramaic-Hebrew words Rouach, Rouah, Rohka, meaning soul.

    *** *** ***

- 11-The Ana'kh word **Asangari** or **Askari** means soldier; warrior. From Asangari, derived the Turkish and Arabic word Askari, which means a soldier. The Ana'kh word Askari appeared in several Semitic and Middle Eastern languages, including Turkish, Swahili, Nabatean, Arabic, Persian, and Somali.

    *** *** ***

- 12- The Ana'kh word **Ashirach**: A prisoner. From Ashirach, derived the Hebrew and Arabic words Asir.

    *** *** ***

- 13- From the Ana'kh word Arda, derived the Hebrew word Eretz, and the Arabic word Ard which mean earth, or soil.

    *** *** ***

- 14- The Ana'kh expression **Baliba nahr usu na Ram**. Translated verbatim: "The water of the river purified my people." Attributed to Sinhar Marduchk in the Book of Rama-Dosh. Baliba means flows of waters. Nahr means river (Same meaning in Hebrew, Phoenician and Arabic).

Usu means to clean or purify.
Na means my or our.
Ram means people (Same meaning in Phoenician, primitive Arabic, early Armenian and ancient Hebrew).
The Ana'kh word "Usu" also means to dig.
We find similar meaning in the Annals of Sardanapalus: "Nahrtu istu nahr zaba anta ahri nahr babilat kanin sumsa abbi." Translated verbatim: "A river from the upper Zab I dug and its name I called."

*** *** ***

- 15-The Ana'kh word **Banati:** Daughters; girls.

From Banati, derived the Assyrian word Banati (Women), the Arabic and Hebrew words Bint and Banat (Girls).

Note: I could cite up to 7,000 Anunnaki's words that created 23,000 equivalent words used today in the Western and Eastern languages, but the book space limitation would not allow me to do so.
Please refer to my books: "Anunnaki Dictionary Thesaurus. Ana'kh: Language of the Extraterrestrial Gods and Goddesses", and "Anunnaki Language and Vocabulary."

*** *** ***

On aliens' abilities of speaking many of our languages:
As to the languages of other extraterrestrial races, and aliens' abilities of speaking many of our languages, Ulema Oppenheimer has said that aliens can record on their Miraya and grids, all the dialects and languages on Earth in a few seconds, code the accents and words pronunciations (Dictions), rewind everything they have recorded, and speak to you in your language. And if they miss a word, they can transmit it to your brain telepathically and you wouldn't know the difference.

*** *** ***

Question #2: Is there a way for us to learn using their methods?

Asnwer:
- 1. Absolutely. There are two Anunnaki-Ulema techniques that allow you to learn many languages in no time.
- 3. The first one is called Jisru, which means bridge in Akkadian, Sumerian, Assyrian, Old Babylonian, Arabic, Ulemite and Ana'kh.
- 2. There is a bridge between all Eastern languages.
- 3. There is a bridge between all Western languages.
- 4. When you cross the bridge, all affiliated languages will be instantly absorbed by your mind.
- 5. The second technique is called "Ilmu or Dirasa Fikriya", which means the mental study. More precisely, the activation of your mind.
- 6. Both techniques will easily allow you to learn up to 24 languages in less than 2 weeks.

*** *** ***

Question #3: It would make the world a much better place if everyone could understand each other.

Answer:
- 1. That is correct.
- 2. But understanding each other is never enough. We should love each other unconditionally.
- 3. And there are two rapid ways to do it:
- a- To start to feel the pleasure in the pleasure of giving;
- b- To forgive as much as you can, and help everybody without restriction, especially those who cannot return the favor.

*** *** ***

46. On super tall beings, Coral Castle, Admiral Byrd, animal mutilations
⌘ ⌘ ⌘

- Question #1: What is known about The Big Boys...the super, super tall beings that are like no other entities?
- Ulema de Lafayette's answer
- Question #2: Who were the beings who lived in the caves in the American southwest which were discovered approx. 100 years ago by the Smithsonian explorer?
- Ulema de Lafayette's answer
- Question #3: Does LaFayette have any theories as to how 'coral castle' was built?
- Ulema de Lafayette's answer
- Question #4: Does LaFayette have any theories as to the meaning of the crop circles?
- Ulema de Lafayette's answer
- Question #5: What is really going on on the moon?
- Ulema de Lafayette's answer
- Question #6: Is there anything to the theories regarding what Admiral Byrd saw from the plane at the South Pole and the reports from places like Mt Shasta?
- Ulema de Lafayette's answer
- Question #7: Who or what is really doing the animal 'mutilations' and for what reason?
- Ulema de Lafayette's answer

46. On super tall beings, Coral Castle, Admiral Byrd, animal mutilations
⌘⌘⌘

Note: Questions from Ms. L., who did not want to reveal her identity, and who asked me not to mention her name in the book.
Questions:
Question #1: What is known about The Big Boys...the super, super tall beings that are like no other entities?

De Lafayette's answer:
- 1. In ancient times, they were called the giants (Biblical Giants), as well as Gibborim, Jababira in Hebrew, Aramaic, Syriac, Assyrian, and Arabic, and Bene ha Elohim by the Habiru (Early Hebrews) and the Jews of Babylon. Alternate names: Anakim, Raphaim, Nephilim, Anunnaki, Anuki, so on.
- 2. In modern day ufology, theories about them are endless, and are not worthy of any discussion. 99.99% of what you read about Anunnaki (Articles, reports, blogs, and personal opinions and vicious attacks on the Anunnaki) are silly and FALSE, even if they were written by famous authors, college professors and so-called authorities in the field.
- 3. There is no such thing as "An authority on the Anunnaki", unless the author of those articles, claims and opinions:

1-Knows very well the Akkadian language;

2-Has demonstrated linguistic expertise in Akkadian, Old Babylonian, Sumerian, and Assyrian languages. This expertise is accepted if the author has taught these languages in accredited institutions, and/or has either deciphered the cuneiform clay tablets, translated them, published his or her translations with reference to the original texts and their transliteration, or simply wrote dictionaries and lexicons on these languages.
How many people do you who have accomplished that?

I do know some, and I have read outstanding work done by illustrious researchers, authors and linguists. But this literary elite vintage has faded away, longtime ago!!

3-Has spent meaningful and extended time (Not less than 5 years) in the Middle East and the Near East, researching, and/or participating in any of the following activities and projects belonging to: archeology, anthropology, regional history, linguistic studies of the modern, ancient and vanished languages of the regions.

4-Has visited museums and institutions of learning displaying the ancient clay tablets, and conferred with curators known for their expertise in the field.

5-Has been trained, oriented and accredited by the Anunnaki-Ulema. Allow me to point out that there are 700 Ulema worldwide, and 200 Anunnaki-Ulema Mounawariin. Have those authors previously mentioned, and those Internet mental cases bloggers, nerds and wacki-wackos been trained by or accepted by the Anunnaki-Ulema, or published any book or dictionary on the languages of the Mesopotamian clay tablets, history religions, culture, folklore, mythology and civilizations of the ancient kingdoms in the Middle East and Near East?
Have they??????
Show me one who is still around!

*** *** ***

Question #2: Who were the beings who lived in the caves in the American southwest which were discovered apx 100 years ago by the Smithsonian explorer?

Ulema de Lafayette's answer:
- 1. They are not extraterrestrials.
- 2. They simply belong to different human races.

*** *** ***

Question #3: Does LaFayette have any theories as to how 'coral castle' was built?

Ulema de Lafayette's answer:
- 1. I am fully convinced that the very loving and the very peaceful, the late Mr. Edward Leedskalnin has built his most unusual castle using levitation.
- 2. One week before he was attacked and murdered by a gang of loosers and drifters, he told Master Sorenztein how he managed to transport his initial castle to where it is located now, and demonstrated to him how the huge stones were lifted.
- 3. It was said that Mr. Edward Leedskalnin has acquired these supernatural powers from learning the Tay Al Ard techniques from the honorable Master Naphtali ben Yacoob, a colleague of the honorable Anunnaki-Ulema Rabbi Mordecai ben Zvi in Latvia. Master Mordecai was born in Latvia.

*** *** ***

Question #4: Does LaFayette have any theories as to the meaning of the crop circles?

Ulema de Lafayette's answer:
- 1. The simple and ugly ones are man-made.
- 2. The ones with quasi academic and popular patterns are made by academicians, skeptics, and "challengers". You know what I mean.
- 3. The ones with spherical and "propagated" designs, forms and patters are made by elements of the nature, including weather, some kind of vortexes, space, atmospheric conditions, and additional anomalies.
- 4. Those which could be equated and/or associated with mathematical symbols and scientific languages are made by intelligent forces, and higher elements that manifest their presence occasionally for the purpose of guiding and stimulating the human intelligence.

*** *** ***

Question #5: What is really going on on the moon?

Ulema de Lafayette's answer:
- 1. Mind-boggling and unbelievable projects, activities and secret operations, I am not allowed to talk about.
- 2. I do not wish to jeopardize and/or threaten my safety, security and sanity!

*** *** ***

Question #6: Is there anything to the theories regarding what Admiral Byrd saw from the plane at the South Pole and the reports from places like Mt Shasta?

Answer:
- 1. Absolutely! More than you think.
- 2. The book "De Lafayette Mega Encyclopedia of UFOs, Extraterrestrials, Aliens Encounters & Galactic Races." contains hundreds of pages on this subject, with mind-bending facts, findings, data and secret reports." Please refer to it.

*** *** ***

Question #7: Who or what is really doing the animal 'mutilations' and for what reason?

Ulema de Lafayette's answer:
- 1. The Grays, and some para-military units.
- 2. Again, I can't talk anymore about this subject.
- 3. I want to be always "welcome" in the United States!
- 3. However, you can still read what I have written on animal mutilations, before I came to the United States.

47. Rekh-get-Amen, and the Anunnaki-Ulema Extraordinary Deeds and Faculties
⌘⌘⌘

I. Definition and introduction
II. Unusual deeds by Anunnaki-Ulema as told by an Ulema novice
1. Introduction: The Anunnaki-Ulema
a- Anunnaki-Ulema, Grand Master Li
b- Anunnaki-Ulema Cheik Al Huseini
c- Anunnaki-Ulema Rabbi Mordechai
II. Stories about the Anunnaki-Ulema
1. Master Li calming down a cobra in the street of Benares
2. Making a bird from paper
3. Master Li feeding the fish and birds with food that came from nowhere
4. The Tuareg and the magical coffee cup
5. Folding the space
6. The amazing deeds of Anunnaki-Ulema Mordechai

47. Rekh-get-Amen, and the Anunnaki-Ulema Extraordinary Deeds and Faculties
⌘⌘⌘

I. Definition and introduction:
Rekh-get-Amen, refers to a group of Anunnaki-Ulema known for their extraordinary deeds and faculties.
In the West, writers interpreted Rekh-get-Amen, as the name of the priests, hierophants, and teachers of magic, who, according to Lenormant, Maspero, the Champollions, etc., etc., "could levitate, walk the air, live under water, sustain great pressure, harmlessly suffer mutilation, read the past, foretell the future, make themselves invisible, calm down snakes, and cure diseases" (Bonwick, Religion of Magic).
And the same author adds: "Admission to the mysteries did not confer magical powers.

These depended upon two things:
- **a**-The possession of innate capacities;
- **b**-The knowledge of formulæ employed under suitable circumstances."

*** *** ***

II. Unusual deeds by Anunnaki-Ulema

1. Introduction: The Anunnaki-Ulema.
The Anunnaki-Ulema are not a homogenous group. They come from various backgrounds, born to parents of diverse religions, and from every country in the world.
None of that matters to them – their affiliation is never to a religion, nor to a country. They are citizens of the world and they serve humanity. The way they serve is not the same. Some

Anunnaki-Ulema are recluses, spending their lives in study and research.
Others live in the world and are very much part of it. For example, the powerful organization, Pères du Triangle, which has enormous influence on world affairs, economics, security, and politics, and is functioning in total secrecy, is manned entirely by people who have had the Anunnaki-Ulema training.

The members are hardly recluses. In the Lodges occupied by the Pères du Triangle, one can meet heads of state, military leaders, Nobel Prize winners, and many other dignitaries who are entirely in the public eye.
All Anunnaki-Ulema share high ethics, unblemished moral behavior, charity, love of animals that includes strict vegetarian diet, service to the poor and helpless, and most interesting – they are all rewarded by a legendary longevity.
Every one of the Masters that Germain Lumière had been taught by was at least a hundred years old, and some were close to two hundred. Nor do they show the signs of age; they are able to choose the age they appear to be, and often change it, which may confuse ordinary people with whom they mingle.

*** *** ***

a- Anunnaki-Ulema, Grand Master Li:
Master Li is Germain Lumière's first teacher. He was born in China, and when we meet him in the book, he is well over a hundred years old, but looks about fifty. He is tall, slim, and has a white beard. Sometimes he wears traditional Chinese robes, sometimes he prefers a European attire – very likely depending on the type of his current mission.
Master Li works in the diplomatic service, sometimes as an ambassador, other times behind the scenes, aiding governments all over the world in the most delicate affairs. His linguistic abilities are legendary, and his turn of mind highly philosophical and extremely calm under all circumstances.
He is also a talented healer and Germain is a witness to his treatment of a very sick woman whom he brings back to complete health – instantaneously.

Though he possesses considerable extrasensory abilities and techniques, Master Li's view of the matter is that if it is possible to do something naturally, it is best to leave it at that and not call on any supernatural agency or power. He does not consort or employ supernatural beings unless absolutely necessary.

*** *** ***

b- Anunnaki-Ulema Cheik Al Huseini:
Living and working in Baalbeck, Lebanon, The Cheik has access to some of the most esoteric and important documents in the world, including *The Book of Rama Dosh*.
He belongs to a different tradition than Germain's other masters. As a Middle Eastern Ulema, he comfortably used all the magical techniques that the Western Ulema are trying to avoid, since they follow a different road, working like scientists and generally preferring a simple life style.
He even employs non-human entities, such as Djinn and Afrit, on a regular basis. Even though his own mode of living is modest, he does occasionally follow the sumptuous tradition of King Solomon.

*** *** ***

c- Anunnaki-Ulema Rabbi Mordechai:
Rabbi Mordechai defies characterization.
He dresses like a rabbi, works as an alchemist, Kabbalist, and linguist in addition to his usual Ulema duties, and while his turn of mind is highly scientific, he is not above creating supernatural beings if he needs them to do some heavy and quick work for his many charity cases.
Mordechai can communicate with animals, create genetically engineered plants without a laboratory, and teleport himself in plain daylight. Larger than life and possessing eyes that are so brilliant that they make people lower their own eyes when talking to him, he is certainly not a recluse. On the contrary, he is a bon-vivant, a great cook, loves to dance, and plays the balalaika like a professional.
He can also drink untold quantities of vodka without any ill effects, and despite strict vegetarianism, believes that caviar is another matter and altogether a gray area ("they are eggs!" he claims).

Always cheerful, there is no adversity that Rabbi Mordechai cannot conquer.
Note: He was born in Russia, and it is well documented that he was older than the last Czar.

*** *** ***

II. Stories about the Anunnaki-Ulema

The Ulema teachers could do extraordinary things with utmost serenity and a nonchalant flair.

1. Honorable Master Li calming down a cobra in the street of Benares:
Note from A. Doudnikova: As told by Germain Lumiere; herewith some excerpts from stories told by Lumiere:

*** *** ***

Lumiere's in his own words:
 The streets were literally lined with people, laying on the ground, wrapped in their sand-colored clothes, the same color as the ground. I could not understand why people had to be so poor as to sleep in the street.
 You could not even tell if the people were dead or alive, and the scene frightened me very much. But soon I realized that no one paid particular attention to the situation.
 Women wearing colorful silk saris, that were as striking as the feathers of tropical birds, wove their way among the bodies on the ground. Westerners, mostly British, did the same, looking very military and imposing.
 Suddenly I saw a horrible thing. A large snake crawled among the people on the ground, slithering here and there. No one moved, allowing the snake to pass. I froze with terror; I never saw a snake, except in the zoo.
 The Master put his hand on my shoulder. "The snake will not hurt you, Germain," he said. He raised his hand, and twisted it around, making a strange sound. This was bizarre.
How could one hand make a sound? Apparently, the snake heard it. It rose vertically to the air, went down again, turned, and left the scene. Many of the poor children came to thank the Master. I realized he was well known around this area.
 "You see, Germain, the snake simply went about his own business. It is not right to assume that he meant to harm anyone and be afraid of him, he had no such intention," the Master said cheerfully. All his lessons were like that. He never said, "Watch, I

am going to do something wonderful now, pay attention." No, he did not want us to pay attention to himself, only to what we could see and learn. And indeed his students, knowing that, never interrupted him but always paid attention, since just being around him was a constant learning experience – and a very pleasant one at that."

*** *** ***

2. Making a bird from paper:
Another story told by Germain Lumiere.

"Eventually, after a few weeks, the Master (Mastor Li) came back. We were very happy to see him, of course.
I was particularly interested in his return, not just because I liked him, but because I saw a mystery or two at the house that I wanted to question him about.

First, I discovered a room which had a closed door. I knew I should not enter, but I did anyway, and to my surprise I saw a very untidy mess of papers, all sizes and colors. I was not comfortable asking anyone else, so when the Master came back, I confessed my spying and asked him what the papers were for. The Master smiled, and said, "Go choose whatever paper you like, any color, any size. Bring two or three pieces."

I picked a few nice pieces and returned. The Master asked, "what would you like to see? A bird, maybe? Shall we have a bird visit us?"

"But birds don't go in houses," I said. "Only if they are lost. I don't want any bird to be frightened and lost."

"Not everything is as it seems," said the Master. "Some birds are not lost, nor are they afraid. They just visit." He quickly made a few folds in one of the papers, a white one, and to my amazement, a neat sculpture of a pigeon was sitting in his hands. I laughed, delighted with the trick.

"And I think a bird likes flowers, doesn't it?" asked the Master.

"Yes, they do," I said with conviction.

The Master made a few folds in another piece of paper, a red one. A rose magically appeared in his hand. I was thrilled, and touched the paper carefully. It was all so lifelike. As I touched the bird, it flew out of the Master's hand. I recoiled, slightly shocked.

"Nothing to be afraid of," said the Master. "Come along." He took me to the garden, and the bird flew after us in a rather business-like manner, as if knowing exactly what it meant to do. In plain day light, the Master gently put the rose on a rose bush. The paper rose immediately turned into a real flower, and the paper bird, now a real, living pigeon, settled on the bush and made distinctive pigeon sounds.

"These two are not lost at all," said the Master. "I think they are very happy." I had to agree. Somehow, the incident, despite its magical and unusual tone, did not frighten me at all. I loved it.

And then came the miracle of the tree. In another room in this large house, around the exit to the garden, and with its door wide open, resided many empty flower pots, with just dirt in them but no plants. Passing by them one day, I asked the master, "Why do you keep all these empty pots?"

"They are made for giant trees that like to live inside the house," said the Master.

"But how can you fit a giant tree inside? They are bigger than the ceiling," I said skeptically.

"Well, I really was remiss in not having a few in the house already," said the Master. "They are very important and bring happiness and luck. Please choose one pot, and let me show you how the biggest tree in the world will fit into it."

"But it can't come into the house by itself," I said.

"No, they don't walk, but we can go out and look for it," said the Master. We went out and stood before a giant pepper tree, covered by feathery leaves and red tiny dots of the pepper spice. A living, thriving, beautiful tree that must have been in the garden for many years.

"This tree?" I asked. "But it is not cut, it is growing! Don't cut it, it may be hurt!"

"Of course I won't hurt the tree. But we needed to choose a special kind of tree, right? That is why we are looking at it. Now come back inside and see what happened," said the Master. We returned into the house, and in the formerly empty pot stood a tiny tree, the exact replica of the giant tree outside, complete with the small red dots of the pepper spice. I stared, speechless.

How did it go into the pot?

"This tree is older than the one outside," said the Master. "As a matter of fact, the giant tree is the baby of this little one, and grew from one of its seeds. Where I am going to take you some day, when we start our serious studies, we don't measure people by their size. We measure them by this," he said, tapping the top of his nose to the top of his forehead, "and by that," tapping a small area around his heart. "Size means nothing."

Gradually, slowly, something was happening to me. I calmed down. Under the peaceful influence of the teacher, the magical occurrences, the friendships I developed, and the newness of the culture, I began to feel more and more confident. Of course, I was not aware of it, until an interesting incident brought it to my six-year-old attention."

*** *** ***

3. Master Li feeding the fish and birds with food that came from nowhere:

Note from A. Doudnikova:
Here Germain Lumiere is telling us a heart-felt story about a most unusual fishing experience he had in the company of his teacher Master Li. Both are visiting a small Chinese village on the beach.

Lumiere said (In his own words):
"We will go about the island and show you how people live here," said the Master. We went down to the small beach. Some boats were on the beach, turned upside down, and the men were repairing them.
Unfortunately, the Master explained, they are so poor, and have so little wood, that sometimes they had to simply patch a boat rather than fix it properly, and endangered themselves when they went to sea. But they had no choice in the matter.
Others were fixing their fishing equipment. I saw that when they fished near the beach, they used nets, and when they fished farther in the water, they used boxes made of rattan or bamboo.
"Would you like to try to fish?" said the Master.
"I have never fished before," I said. "What would you use, a net or a box?"

"Neither," said the Master. We went to the edge of the sea. Soft little waves touched the rocks that lined the beach like a natural pier.

"You can take your shoes off so they won't get wet, but don't put your feet or play in the water for a little while," said the Master. "We don't want to scare the fish." He sat on a rock, rolled up his sleeves, and put his finger in the water. He held nothing in his hands.

I watched, fascinated, as the fish started to come to his finger, stuck their little heads up and opened their mouths. From somewhere, I can't imagine where, the Master produced quite a lot of crumbs, and fed the fish.

That was the Master's idea of fishing; he never killed an animal in his life. When he was done, and the fish left, I grabbed his hand to see if there was any mysterious object in it, something with which he called the fish to his fingers. But there was nothing in his hands, nothing in his sleeves.

The Master laughed. "No, I have nothing in my hands, Germain. It is simply knowing how to use your hands properly. Do you know how to join your hands?"

"Yes," I said, and grasped my hands together.

"There is a better way," said the Master. He leaned his closed fist inside his other hand, which was open. "You see, Germain, the fist, which you make with the right hand, is for strength and power. The left hand, left open, is the shield. By holding the fist and the shield together, you protect others from your own aggression."

I tried it, and he approved of the way I placed the hands. "Now," he said, "I am going to teach you how to use the hands, followed by your body, to do what we call 'ballet with nature.' I would like you to practice it every day. Would you do that? And later, when we meet again, I will show you the next step."

"Sure," I said. "How do you ballet with nature?"

"First, you move your left arm in circular motion. Let your body flow with it, your whole body; sway and turn with it. When you get tired, move the arm in the same way, only in the opposite direction."

I tried, and it felt very nice both ways.

"Now, take the right hand, make a fist, and repeat the same dancing motion, first in this direction, then the other." I tried, and again, found it easy. Then I combined the two motions, under his instructions, and he approved. I promised I would do it every day, which I faithfully did. I honestly thought I was dancing... only later I found out, when it was necessary and urgent, that the Master, the gentle, loving Master, really taught me the first rules of deadly self defense, and it would be rather handy later in life.

In the meantime, we returned to the temple. There were a few birds on the shore, not many. To my surprise, they took a look at the Master, and a couple of them flew straight at him and sat on his shoulder. The Master produced more crumbs from thin air, and the birds had their lunch. How did they know he could feed them, I wondered. "They just know," said the Master. "You will find that animals understand more than people do, if you love them."

I have learned so much and enjoyed my stay in the island, but unfortunately we could not stay as long as we wished.

*** *** ***

4. The Tuareg and the magical coffee cup:
Note from A. Doudnikova:
Germain Lumiere and his teacher are now in Damascus (Capital of Syria) visiting an old friend of Master Li.
Here is Germain Lumiere's story in his own words:

Two years after we arrived in Damascus, I was playing in the garden. One of the servants came out and told me, "We have some Chinese people in the house. They want to see you." I had no idea who they could be, and went into the house, rather surprised.

As soon as I crossed the threshold, I froze, noticing a faint, delicate scent of amber mixed with flowers in the air. Only one person on earth was associated with this unique scent combination.

I instantly knew the Master came for me. I ran to him and we hugged each other, I was so happy to see him, I missed him so much.

Suddenly I realized that he looked different – he was dressed in a European suit, not his usual Chinese robes. "And won't you say hello to my wife?" he said, laughing. I looked at the woman who stood nearby, smiling, and did not recognize her.

Who was this lady, dressed like an elegant European, wearing makeup and perfume? She laughed at my amazement and I suddenly recognized my old friend and was delighted to see her. The first thought that crossed my mind was "Thank Heaven we fixed the toilets..."

They loved the house, and we gave them a beautiful room on the second floor. They planned to stay a week or so, and I spent all the time I could with the Master, while his wife went with Mama to various shops and places of interest.

I was hoping he would mention a new trip, but as the visit took place in the middle of the school year, I knew it was not likely to happen. But this was the Master, so I knew something wonderful was bound to happen even if we stay put.

And indeed it happened.

A couple of days later, the Master told me he wanted to introduce me to some important people. I did not know what to expect, and was rather surprised when he headed toward the *suk*, as they called the market. What kind of important people could we meet at the suk (Souk), I wondered, but said nothing and waited to see what was going to happen.

I always loved visiting the suk. It was an extensive, ancient marketplace, part of it in the open air, the other part, which was my favorite, made up of narrow streets under massive arches of stone that served as a roof. Each arch had carvings on it, either pictures or letters, half rubbed off with age. The ground was covered with old, irregular stone slabs.

The stores were narrow, each like a hole in the wall and secured with heavy wooden doors. Many were very small, like tiny caves. Others, though still narrow, were long and burrowed deep into the buildings.

Even during daytime the suk was dark, so yellow lamps shed intimate, golden light over the merchandise. Everything burst with deep, glowing, jewel-toned colors.
Most of the vendors spread or hung the colorful objects around the entrance, to entice the customers to come in.

Anything and everything was sold there – handmade rugs, silk and cotton clothes, accessories, cosmetics, spices, pickles, sacks of rice, beans, sugar, and coffee – anything you could think of.

Copperware shone softly under the glowing lights, wood and leather furniture, inlaid with shells and mother-of-pearl, were piled with gorgeous silver jewellery,
musical instruments produced a faint sound as the people pushed against them, and the scents of coffee, spices, food, and heavy perfumes lingered in the air. It was a place of magic.

We entered a shop that sold beautiful copperware and furniture made of wood and inlaid with mother-of-pearl. Inside, he said a few words in Arabic to the man who was sitting at the shop.

This was the first time I heard him speak Arabic; how many languages did the Master speak, I wondered.

The Arab took us to the back of the shop, to a little room behind a curtain. We entered, and inside sat a most imposing man, wearing a blue Tuareg outfit and a large turban.

He was old and his beard was white, and to me he looked like a mixture of a rabbi, a priest, and a patriarch, very different from the sheiks and the clerics we saw in the street. I sensed that he was very special.

As they were greeting each other in Arabic, I was surprised that the Tuareg did not rise. Arabs are extremely polite and hospitable, and it is unusual that a host would not get up to greet a guest.

The Master introduced me, and we sat on a low divan across a little table from the Tuareg. He offered us coffee, and one of the workers in the shop came in with a tray, and poured it into three tiny cups.

The Master and our host took their drink without sugar, but I could not drink Turkish coffee like that since I found it very bitter, and so I put some sugar into it.

When I finished my coffee, the Tuareg asked me to give him my cup. He shook it a few times, allowing the coffee grounds and sugar to spread themselves around the cup, and said, smiling, "I am going to read your future."

He started by telling me about my past, and what I was doing now, all perfectly accurate. He proceeded to tell me a few things about my doings in the future, then put the cup on the table. I was terribly curious.

What was in the cup that could tell him so much? So I stood up to pick the cup, but the Tuareg said, "no need to move, the cup will come to you if you want it, since you are such a good boy." The Master said, "he really is a good boy," which made me very proud, but before I could thank him, the cup rose in the air and floated toward me, and landed on in my lap. I looked at the Tuareg with speechless amazement.

"We call this Tay Al Ard," said the Tuareg. "It means, folding of the Earth." I did not know what to say, having never heard the term. "You can pick up the cup now," said the Tuareg. "What do you want to do with it?"

"I just want to see the things you saw when you told me about the past and the future," I said. I looked inside, but the cup contained nothing more than some coffee grounds and a bit of sticky sugar.

"There is only coffee mud inside!" I said, disappointed.

"Look again," said the Tuareg.

I looked. The cup became very heavy. I put it in my lap, and the mud inside started to move and fold, like a living creature. I gazed at it, fascinated, but did not know what it meant.

"Can I take it home and show it to my mother?" I said. The cup flew again and went to the table. No, it did not want to go home with me.

The Master said, "This is your first lesson." I had no idea what he meant, and the two of them started to speak in a language I have never heard before. Then the Master rose and told me it was time to leave. The Tuareg said goodbye to me, very kindly, and I noticed that again he did not rise.

In the street, I asked the Master, "Why did he not get up? This is unusual, and in every other way he was so polite and kind."

"He has been sitting like this for thirty years, Germain."

"So he never leaves this room?" I asked, incredulously.

"He does leave the room when he goes to teach in a very special school, which we call Ma'had. He teleports himself."

"He can do that? He can fly through the air? Really?"

"He can do many unusual things. But he cannot walk."

"What happened to him, Master?"

"Years ago, he had an accident and became paralyzed. He was offered two options by some very special people. He could save his body and walk again, or lose his body and acquire knowledge. He chose knowledge and was initiated by these people into a secret order of great scholars."

"Who were they, Master?"

"They were Ulema, Germain, and he is an Ulema as well. The Ulema are teachers of very secret and important knowledge."

"And he lost his ability to walk?"

"His body was cut in half, Germain. He has no lower body at all."

"No lower body? He is just a half of a person?"

"Yes, he is just a half. That is why he cannot rise to greet his guests."

"So how does he live? How does he eat?"

"He does not need to eat. He could, perhaps, if he wanted to, but he has no reason too."

"But he drank coffee! Does he go to the bathroom?" The Master laughed. "No, he does not need to go to the bathroom. Anything he drinks evaporates from his body. When you have Tay Al Ard, you don't need a physical presence. It is no longer of any importance."

I walked along, deep in thought. "Master," I finally said, "you said it was my first lesson. I suppose you mean the Tay Al Ard, but this is not so. It was not my first lesson." The Master gave me a quick, searching look.

"What was your first lesson, then?" he asked quietly.

"The paper bird that you made in Benares. The one that became a real bird and flew to the paper rose that also became a real flower and attached itself to the rosebush."

"I see," said the Master. "So you figured it all out."

"Yes, I think so," I said. I did not add what I have realized, and knew with an assurance that cannot be explained, then or now. There was no need to say anything. The Master knew that I understood that he, too, was an Ulema, and that he was doing me the inconceivable honor of teaching me and giving me his friendship.

Why did he choose me?

What have I done to deserve such happiness?

I had no idea. I was only twelve years old, so I could not tell where it started, and what all this would lead to in the future, but I knew one thing with an absolute certainty – I was the luckiest boy in the world.

*** *** ***

5. Folding the space:
Germain Lumiere continues:

"Tay Al Ard," said the Master, "is the metaphysical experience that produces a teleportation phenomenon."

"Would I be able to do it?" I asked. I envisioned myself hopping at will to every corner of the earth, not even bothering to pack.

"Perhaps some day. It is extremely complicated and sometimes even dangerous. For the moment, I just want you to understand the concepts."

"Were did the teachings come from?"

"The Ulema learned it from Rou-hi-yin, who are supreme beings that dwell in the fifth dimension. For many years, they practiced peacefully all over the world.

When Islam came to the Middle East, the Prophet Muhammad banned Tay Al Ard, and many of the Ulema teachers became Allamah, prominent figures in letters, literature, science, and religion.

However, not all of them renounced their Ulema identity. Those who chose to remain Ulema, remained the custodians of the Anunnakis' secret knowledge and esoteric powers.

They joined the circle of Non-Muslim Ulema and the groups shared their knowledge. This was common particularly among the Sufis."

"What do the words Tay Al Ard mean?" I asked.

"The words mean 'the folding of space.' To put it simply, you traverse the earth without moving. Instead of physically moving from one place to another, the enlightened persons do the exact opposite. They bring the place they want to reach to where they stand. The very earth of the place that they wanted to reach actually moves, and is placed under their feet."

"Can you see the earth as it moves?"

"Never. It happens in a blink of an eye, no matter how far the destination is."

"And only the Ulema know how to do it, Master?"

"That depends how you look at it. Under other names, the phenomenon manifests itself in many other cultures. But some say that all of the great people who practiced Tay Al Ard, such as the great king Solomon from Judea, were secret Ulema anyway. It is well known that King Solomon moved the throne of the Queen of Sheba to his own palace so that she would feel at home during her visit with him. The event was recorded by both Islamic and Jewish teachings."

"Are there any scientific explanations as to how it works?" I asked. The Master smiled. He saw I was already going in the right direction, and it pleased him.

"This is a very good question," He said. "It was once well put by the Ulema Cheik Al Kabir. His exact words were: Time is represented with two lines not perfectly aligned; one for you, the other for what is not you. Space is represented with two circles, one for you, the other for what is not you.

If you manage to place yourself between one of the two lines and one of the two circles without touching the other line and the other circle, you will conquer time-space."

I considered this. "But time is not going in two lines, Master. It goes straight from yesterday to tomorrow, through today, in one line."

"That is what most people think, but they are wrong, and great thinkers understand the malleability of time and space. Sufis, Gnostics, pre-Islamic, Islamic, and Jewish scholars, all wrote about it. The Jewish Kabbalists, in particular, engaged themselves in the study of Tay Al Ard, but had a different name for it, in Hebrew.

They called it *Kefitzat Haderach*, meaning, word by word, 'the jumping of the road,' but translated as the ability to jump instantaneously from one place to another or travel with unnatural speed. It was widely documented by them."

"What about modern scientists?" I asked.

"Einstein discussed it in a number of his papers, and it was a component of his General Relativity Theory, relating to the warping of space-time enabled by the effects of gravity."

"I read fairy tales and science fiction stories about such things," I said.

"Of course you did. Fiction writers have been using it for many years," said the Master. "But it is based on truth."

"But I still don't understand the principle of it," I said. "How does the earth jump?"

"There are many explanations," said the Master, "none of them complete, since mysteries are sometimes only partially understood. Look at it this way. Newtonian physics, which did not allow such occurrences, were replaced long ago. Such things as wormholes, dark matter, and space-time fluidity allow much more flexibility in investigating teleportation. It is complicated.

For example, Quantum physics has proven that particles, such as photons and atoms, can appear instantaneously at a new place without traveling through space in any visible manner.
Perhaps this phenomenon is possible by encoding information about an object, transmitting the information to another place, and creating a copy of the original in the new location."

"In this solution, then, the earth does not jump."

"This is correct. But in both explanations the physical phenomenon is similar, as it is based on the disintegration of the atoms, those of the earth or those of the person, and their reassembly at the place of destination. I see no true conflict here."

"In the stories I read, the person just wishes to go somewhere, and there he goes," I said.

"Again, this is not a contradiction," said the Master. "In Western science it is now assumed that space does not have an objective reality, and reality itself is thought of as observer-based and subjective entity.

If so, then ideas such as traveling in space without actually physically moving are no longer so strange. In this way, Tay Al Ard is viewed as the manipulation of reality by the person who wishes to travel from point one to point two in an environment that is subject to the traveler's will."

"And so," I said, "the idea is everywhere, stories, science, different cultures, and you know many people who have done it. I suppose you have done it too."

"Yes, I have," said the Master.

"Well, then," I said, "why can't I learn to do it right away?"

"Because a child might be hurt in some of the places you might want to jump to, Germain. If the environment is not safe, and you are even a little bit confused by it, you won't be able to find your way out and may even be killed. Let's wait until you are an adult."

"Ah, well," I said resignedly. "I guess the trip I was planning to the South Pole, to visit the penguins, must be postponed."

"Just a few years," said the Master.

*** *** ***

6. The amazing deeds of Anunnaki-Ulema Mordechai:
Note from A. Doudnikova:
Ulema Mordechai, a father figure to Germain Lumiere, and his second Anunnaki-Ulema teacher came to visit with his mother, the French Marquise and Germain in Paris, France.
Germain Lumiere is telling us wonderful stories about the extraordinary deeds and things his teacher could do.

Lumiere said, verbatim:
Indeed. No one who had met Rabbi Mordechai even once could forget him, anymore that you could forget an earthquake or a typhoon. His energy, love of life, and powerful personality would leave strong impression immediately on anyone who had the pleasure of meeting him.

I remembered him very well, a large man with a long white beard, with a booming voice and a hearty laugh, always cheerful, always pleasant. I knew I would recognize him right away, and looked forward to it. I went to Mama to inquire and she said, "Have I forgotten to tell you? How could I? I must really be too busy if I could do that. It will be such fun to see Rabbi Mordechai again."

Two weeks later, around seven o'clock at night, I came home from school. As soon as I opened the door, I heard a laugh that filled the entire house, and I knew Rabbi Mordechai came. The house felt different, as if the quiet atmosphere was charged by some extra energy that was not there before.

I heard him calling me from the other room, booming at me as soon as I closed the door, though how he knew it was me I could never understand. "Finally you are here! I could not wait to see you!"

And a great big bear of a man rushed out of the living room and hugged me with incredible strength. He let me go, held me at arm's length, and looked at me with his intense blue green eyes, so bright that some people had difficultly looking at them and would lower their own eyes when he looked at them.

He did not change at all, the white beard, long and thick, almost reached his belt, and he still wore the dark suit that was his signature. I remember him telling me that people who saw him from the back, wearing this black coat, thought he was a priest, but as soon as he turned, they would realize he must be a rabbi, but then again, not quite...to me he looked like the personification of a Russian peasant, but highly intellectual. Rabbi Mordechai was not easy to categorize.

"You look well, my boy" he said, and I felt that his approval was important, and was very happy to hear it. "You look wonderful too, Rabbi," I said. "I am so happy to see you again."

"Don't think that just because I did not see you for a few years, I did not know what you were doing," said Rabbi Mordechai. "Our friend, Master Li, kept me abreast of your advancement. He is very pleased with it." A sudden suspicion occurred to me that their connections with each other, and also with me and my mother, were not accidental, but I did not know at that time how to connect the dots, so I let it pass.

"I see you are still wearing your ring, Rabbi," I said, laughing. I used to be fascinated with his ring. It was a heavy ring set with a green topaz, which could be opened to reveal a secret compartment. Inside, he kept a dry bean, on which he wrote, in miniature, the entire Torah. "Is the bean still there?" I continued. "Of course," said Rabbi Mordechai. "I need the Torah with me all the time."

"And where have you been all these years?"

"Mostly in Estonia and Lithuania," he said. "So much help is needed under the Soviets... such poor people, starving, homeless. I built towns for them."

"You built towns?" I asked, incredulously. How could one man build towns?

"Oh yes, I'll tell you about it later," he said casually. "It's a long story, and we should not keep your mother waiting."

We returned to the living room, where Mama was pouring out some drinks for us to have before we went in for dinner. "Now, my dear Madame Lumière, don't you think you need a mezuzah? Where is your mezuzah? I did not see one when I came in."

"Please, Rabbi, with all due respect, I don't need any religious objects in this house," said Mama, sighing, and handed him his drink. "They never did me much good, to say the least."

"Ah, you will think differently about the kind of mezuzah I am talking about..." and he pulled out of his pocket a mezuzah and put it on the table. It was covered by blue and white diamonds of the first quality. Mama picked it up and looked at it, amazed.

"Well!" she said, "Perhaps I should change my mind... Shall I put it in my bedroom? It won't be safe to keep a thing like that on the front door."

"You can't even carry it to your bedroom, Madame Lumière," he said, his blue green eyes twinkling with amusement. "It's much too heavy."

I saw Mama looking at the mezuzah that she was still holding in total amazement. It seemed to be pushing her hand down, getting heavier and heavier. She placed it on the table, unable to hold it any longer. I tried to pick it up, and Rabbi Mordechai said, "Didn't you learn anything in Damascus? Don't you remember what happened when you tried to grab such a thing?"

I suddenly remembered the coffee cup I drank from when I visited the Tuareg in the suk in Damascus, as a child. The mezuzah had to be the same type of enchanted object, with a mind of its own.

Rabbi Mordechai looked at the mezuzah, and just like the cup, it jumped into my lap. I did not touch it, and did not quite know what to do.

What's more, I was a little uncomfortable about his knowledge regarding my visit to the Tuareg. How did he know? I looked at him with some suspicion and he burst out laughing, and gently slapped my face. "I know a lot of things," he said. "I told you, I have watched over your advancement for years."

Mama ignored this exchange and said, "Why don't you take care of my arthritis instead of playing such tricks, if you are so powerful? I could not hold on to it, it was too heavy for my arms."

"This has nothing to do with arthritis, it really is just a trick of sorts. You can put it back on the table, Germain, it won't bite." I did and he put it back in his pocket, and we went to dinner.

After dinner, Mama, who was extremely tired after a long day at work, excused herself and retired to her own room. Rabbi Mordechai and I went to the library. "Now, he said, "let's go back to the issue of the mezuzah, shall we? Look." He took it out of his pocket and gave it to me. It was definitely the same mezuzah, but not a single diamond remained on it, and it seemed to be made of copper. "You see, using these tricks was the way I could help those poor people in Estonia and Lithuania. I can change metals, and other substances, into gold, diamonds, or other precious stones, as needed."

"So you put the diamonds in the mezuzah for a limited period of time?"

"Not exactly. I did not really have to put them in. When performing this trick, the person involved usually sees the physical object or property he or she lost and could not regain. Your mother lost her diamonds in the war, and her vision of the diamonds affected the mezuzah.

You never lost anything of a material nature, so now, while not influenced by her vision, you are seeing plain metal. It's much like a crystal ball. People see different things when they look into the same crystal ball, since it reflects their minds. If you were ill, you would see something related to illness and recovery. Had your mother's arthritis been really bad, she would have seen something related to it, rather than the diamonds. Fortunately, her arthritis is very mild.

I needed to build houses for the people in Estonia and Lithuania. Most of the people from whom I needed to buy materials or get licenses, lost money in the past.

So if I put anything on the table in front of them, lets say some leaves, or paper, they saw money, took it, and let me have anything I needed."

"And would the money disappear?"

"Sometimes, but not in a way that could incriminate me. Also, if they were good people, they could keep it."

I was silent. Something strange was happening here, I thought. Why is he telling me all these things? There had to be some plan, some pattern, to his sudden appearance...

"I am going to give you this mezuzah," he said. "Carry it with you. When you are in trouble, real trouble, look at it, and you may be able to see the solution to your problem.

It has a great secret, look." He held it in his hand, and with the other hand, opened an invisible compartment, then closed it. "Now," he said, "Try to open it."

I took the mezuzah and there was simply no compartment to be found. The mezuzah was seamless. I looked at him with amazement.

"The compartment will only open three times in your lifetime. It will grant you three wishes. One of them, the last one, will be the ultimate request, relating to life and death. Before that, one wish will be used for yourself, the other for someone else. If you ask for help and the compartment opens, this is the sign that the wish will be granted. Now take it and put it in your pocket."

"Rabbi Mordechai," I said, putting the mezuzah in my pocket, "You have great powers, don't you?"

"I plan to teach you a great deal of these powers," he said without elaborating. "Now, off to sleep! I am an old man and it is three o'clock in the morning!"

I could not sleep, this was really exciting.

Why was Rabbi Mordechai planning to teach me?

Was this the plan?

What about the Master?

There were so many questions. But before trying to resolve anything else, I decided I had to find out what this mysterious mezuzah was made of.

I had a friend in the Institut Pasteur, a scientist, who in turn had a friend who worked in a military lab. Next morning, my friend and I went to the lab, and let the military man look at it. He took preliminary measurements, so as to coordinate weight to size, and then put the mezuzah on a scale, matching it to a light weight that should have worked against a small copper object. But it did not work.

To our surprise, the mezuzah's side of the scales sank down immediately as if it were much heavier than the weight. The military man fixed the scales and tried again, with the same results.

"This object is registering 20 kilograms," he said. "But it cannot be. A small object made of copper could not weigh that much under any circumstances. I don't know how to proceed." My friend from the Institut Pasteur picked it up, and it was extremely light again. "This is bizarre," said my friend. "No point in going on, it won't work. Let's go home."

I took the mezuzah home. Rabbi Mordechai was there, and somehow he knew where I was.

I can't imagine how he knew, since I told no one at home about my plans, but eventually I got used to his ability to find out where I went. He looked sad. "That was not good, son. You could have asked me any questions you wanted about the mezuzah, but instead you went to the military.

That is not good." he seemed upset about it and I felt like a real fool and apologized. "Well," he said, "never mind. Put on your hat and coat. I have got something to show you. We are going to visit an old friend of mine, I often stay with him when I am in Paris."

We went to a small house in a quiet side street near Avenue Victor Hugo, and a pleasant little man opened the door and greeted us warmly. Rabbi Mordechai introduced him as Mr. Markowitch. He took us into a modest living room, and opened a bottle of Calvados.

We sat comfortably, sipping our drinks, and Rabbi Mordechai said, "Son, not even the biggest scientist in France knows as much as this gentleman who is right here with us."

Mr. Markowitch smiled in a deprecating way, and said, "No, no. I am nothing special..."

Rabbi Mordechai waved his hand, dismissing Mr. Markowitch's modesty. "I say, my friend, would you mind showing your laboratory to Germain?"

Not at all," said Mr. Markowitch. "I will be delighted to show it to him." We went into the basement, which was large and comprised of several rooms. Mr. Markowitch opened a door, and stood aside to let up pass.

What I saw there was in such complete contradiction to the simple living room that I gasped.

The room was a combination of a movie set and a medieval laboratory, large, messy, dusty, and full of tubes, flasks, bottles, boiling water, and steam.

I smelled something boiling, burning metals, and other strange odors. What in the world was this? Suddenly I had a hunch. "Are you an alchemist?" I asked, bewildered.

"Not cxactly," said Mr. Markowitch. "I am only a transmutist, though I do my best to work for the benefit of humanity. Rabbi Mordechai is an alchemist, though. The greatest alchemist I have ever known." That was something to digest. I knew Rabbi Mordechai was many things, but an alchemist was not something I expected.

"There is a difference? Don't both professionals try to transmute metals?" I asked.

"Yes and no. The alchemists are of a higher level. They can transmute metals into pure gold, and also can produce the Elixir of Life. The transmutists can change substances into any metal other than gold, and we cannot manufacture the Elixir of Life."

"I see," I said, not quite sure if I understood the implications.

"Look at this," said Mr. Markowitch. He opened a drawer of a big table and took out a chunk of raw gold. He looked at it affectionately. "This is Rabbi Mordechai's first gift to me," he said. "The first of many. I would not sell this one for anything... he did not even have a bank account at the time, would you believe it? And he produced this beautiful gold for me. He never thinks about himself."

"So what do you do, Mr. Markowitch?" I asked, curious.

"I work for a French-Swiss pharmaceutical company as a chemist. That is my regular job. But I am also trying to work for myself, by creating a formula for a wonderful perfume.

Rabbi Mordechai helped me all along, and if everything turns out well I will be able to make a lot of money. That would be so nice. Anyway, let Rabbi Mordechai show you his own workshop, which he uses whenever he comes to Paris."

He went upstairs, and we entered Rabbi Mordechai's room, which stood in complete contrast to his friend's medieval lair. No tubes, no containers of any sort, nothing was boiling or steaming in this room. On the left side he had a large, old fashioned wooden table. Next to it stood a machine with a glass top, the likes of which I have never seen.

A bed stood under an arch window. Next to it was placed a large sofa. On the right side stood two tall bookcases, and between them, a metal armoire, entirely modern, unlike the wooden country table.

I commented on the lovely Bohemian crystal chandelier, and Rabbi Mordechai told me he got it in Yugoslavia.

"Shall we have some coffee?" asked Rabbi Mordechai. He went to a kitchenette-like corner, fitted with a few shelves and a sink, and started preparing strong Turkish coffee.

Settling comfortably in his chair and sipping his coffee, Rabbi Mordechai said, "And now, I promised to tell you the story of the houses I built. Do you want to hear it?"

"Oh, yes, I do," I said. "I am not sure what you mean by building houses. I had no idea you worked in this line."

"Well, I built houses, but I never laid my hands on a stone or a brick," he said, his bright eyes twinkling with amusement.

"So you supervised their construction? Like an architect?"

"Well, maybe it could be described this way... You will be the judge. You see, the people I wanted to help were poor peasants. They had no money at all, they ate meat once a year, maybe, and some of them lived in groups of eight to ten in one small shack. I decided I had to build them more houses, give them decent living conditions.

Luckily, there was a piece of land in the vicinity that did not belong to anyone. I went to look at it, make sure there was water around so we could dig a good well.

I found plenty of water, decided it was the right place, and then, boom! Overnight, I built them ten houses. Come to think of it, I had some preliminary preparations to do, so it really was not exactly overnight, but more like twenty-four hours."

"But it takes more than twenty-four hours to build even a single room, let alone ten houses! Did you have hundreds of people to help you?"

"The work was done by four individuals and one enormous blanket," said Rabbi Mordechai. "Getting them was what I referred to as preliminary preparations."

"Did you say blanket, Rabbi Mordechai, or did I misunderstand you? What does a blanket have to do with building houses?"

"No, you heard me right. The four individuals did not wish to be observed as they were building the houses."

I sat there, watching him a bit suspiciously. Was he trying to confuse me, see how I would react to this fairytale? Or perhaps it was some sort of a test? Or maybe I was just so stupid that I did not understand?

Rabbi Mordechai looked at me and said, "I can see that you feel that four are not enough to build ten houses overnight, right?"

"No way," I said.

"For a really important good cause, Germain, I can use one individual to build something bigger than the Eiffel Tower, and in seconds."

Rabbi Mordechai was never drunk. My mother told me that he was a real "Russian bear" and could polish a whole bottle without any effects. So obviously he could not be drunk now, when all I saw him take was Turkish coffee.

But for a few moments I seriously suspected that he was. Nor was he crazy.

So what nonsense was he telling me? And then I suddenly remembered something that Mr. Markowitch said.

Rabbi Mordechai, he said, was an alchemist. It had little to do with building houses, but still, as an alchemist, he had powers. And then something else connected to it in my mind.

He never said his helpers were four people. He said they were four individuals. Could these individuals be like the Afrit I saw in Baalbeck?

The thought was so sudden, so disturbing, that I was startled and looked at him with apprehension, and I think he read my mind because he said, "No, they are not what you think. Not like those you saw in Baalbeck, anyway. There are other sorts, you know."

"I had no idea that you knew about my meeting with the Afrit," I said. "How did you know I was thinking about them, anyway? Do you read my mind?"

"No, no. I don't read your mind, but what you thought was very clear and showed on your face. The Master told me all about your education, remember?

And I know that the first meeting with the Afrit would make a strong impression on anyone. Anyway, my individuals were much better than the Afrit you met. All Afrit are basically stupid, but mine, at least, listened and obeyed."

"Are they spirits, are they humans, part human? What are they?" I asked.

"Mine are called *Ghooliim*."

"This strange name sounds somewhat familiar," I said, "but I can't quite place it."

"Yes, you are right, and this is a very good observation! I am pleased to see that you can make good connections in your mind.

Indeed, the Ghooliim are part animal, part human, part Golem, part Ghoul. A hybrid race. They are made of clay, or earth materials, much like you and me, but they have certain physical differences from both humans and animals. For example, they are born full adult. They are sensitive to light, by the way, so they work only by night, but they are nevertheless great engineers."

"Where do you find them?" I asked.

"I make them," said Rabbi Mordechai.

"You make them? Really? So they are like machines? Robots?"

"They look exactly like you and me, they have eyes, hands, feet, etc. They are not at all like machines or robots. You will not think them anything but human if you saw them."

I leaned forward in my chair, shaken by what I was beginning to understand. Can he do the impossible, can he be playing God? "So you actually create living, breathing, thinking creatures? The Afrit I met where merely conjured spirits, but you are talking about something else, I think. A different level of beings."

"When the Ulema, and some Kabbalists, reach the holy level of Kadash *Daraja*, they can create life.

Real life. The creatures would function much like human beings, but they have three deep fundamental differences. They don't have a soul, they don't have a physical heart that functions like a blood pump, and they don't have a wired brain. Also, their essence comes from another dimension, to which they return after their task is done.

They are created for that task, and that is their only purpose. The creator tells them what to do, and they do it right away. In my case, I have created these four Ghooliim to build the houses, and they did it very nicely, overnight."

"Can you tell me how you create them?"

"I create each of the Ghooliim separately. For each, I bring with me seven pieces of papers on which I write certain codes, and I have to have my cane with me. Then I take soil, earth, or clay, and pour water on it to make it pliable. Once it's the right consistency, I mold it into a ball.

I turn off most of the lights, leaving a very low illumination, maybe one candle or a small lamp, and pull back about four to five feet. I then read a certain text that would encourage the ball to take the next step, which is to shape itself into an oblong of about four feet, and be ready to follow my special design.

At that point I take my cane, walk to the other side of the oblong, dip the cane into the oblong, and stretch it. I command the oblong to duplicate a human form, and it becomes a statue, lifeless, but similar in every way to the human form.

I take the seven pieces of paper, and put two in the eyes, two in the ears, one in the mouth, and one on the breast, over the heart. I roll the seventh piece as if it were a homemade cigarette, go to the other side of the statue, and throw the rolled paper at it.

It always lands either in the nose or between the feet, and either position is correct.

The statue starts to move and attempts to stand up. At this time I turn around and leave the room for a few minutes, so as not to look at the statue as it comes to life. Seeing the actual transformation is forbidden by the Code of the Ulema, as stated in the Book of Rama Dosh.

I stand behind the door of the room, and wait until I hear the creature make a sound, which tells me that the procedure is complete. I go back into the room, welcome the creature, give it clothes to wear, and pull out all the papers, to keep safely until such time as they are needed to disassemble the creature and send its essence back to its original dimension."

"And you do that after the task is done."

"Right, since the Ghooliim are created to perform a single task. When the task is accomplished, I ask the Ghooliim to lie on the floor, next to each other, return the pieces of paper with the codes to the correct places, and pour water over the bodies of the Ghooliim. The bodies disappear, leaving earth on the floor, and the essence goes back to where it came from."

"Do they always go away peacefully?" I asked.

"No, sometimes they develop a personality, if the task is a bit longer, and they have the delusion of being human and want to stay in our dimension. Of course it would be cruel and inhuman to let them stay, not to mention dangerous, but they do become tricky.

So the Ulema or Kabbalist must be even trickier, and hypnotize the creature into deep sleep. We then put the papers where they belong and set the paper on fire, and the body start smouldering. At that time, we pour the water over the Ghooliim and they disappear."

"Fascinating," I said. "I would love to witness the procedure, though I admit some of it would be terrifying. Thinking of the creature stumbling to its feet, trying to get up, in a dark room... still, I wish I could witness that.

"You will do better than just witnessing. At the right time I will teach you the whole process, including the codes and the text that needs to be said," promised Rabbi Mordechai.

"I will know how to create life? Really?" I said incredulously.

"Why not? Once initiated, you will advance. I tell you, think big! Expect everything! Grow! That is what I hope you will do. Anyway, the houses were built very nicely by these obliging Ghooliim."

"And then?"

"The next morning, very early, I went to inspect the houses, and removed the great blanket that covered the area."

"What is this blanket?" I asked. "We are not talking about a real blanket, right?"

"No, it is a large plasmic sheet that can create a shield of invisibility over the entire area. We just refer to it as a 'blanket' because it's a short and easy name. Anyway, someone saw the houses and informed the police, and soon enough I saw them advancing on me. Luckily, the captain was an old friend, Sergei, and he had two policemen with him.

"'What is this?' he asked me, surprised. He knew the area well and these houses did not exist the day before.

'These are houses,' I said.

'Well, I see that, but how come? How did you occupy the land, how did you build, and what about a license? Surely you don't have one? And who did you build it for? You know very well that you will have to abandon this property right away, you have no right to it,' said Sergei.

'Sergei, my friend, you are asking too many questions...' I said. 'When your wife was dying, and the doctors gave up on her, do you remember who saved her life?'

'Why, it was you, Rabbi Mordechai,' said Sergei. 'Do you think I would ever forget that? Or my wife, for that matter? She never stops praising your name.'

'And did you ask any questions then? No, you were too happy to see her well. And anyway, if you had asked, I would not know how to explain it to you.'

'You just touched her, and she stood up,' said Sergei. 'It looked like a miracle, so I did not want to interfere...'"

That rang a bell. I remembered something. "Wait!' I said to Rabbi Mordechai, interrupting his narrative. 'That is exactly what the Master did for the sick nun, Sister Marie-Ange Gabrielle, who stayed in our house many years ago, before we went to Damascus...'

"Very likely," said Rabbi Mordechai. "I am sure no one asked too many questions then, either. Anyway, I told Sergei that I have done much more than just touch his wife, and I put my hand on his shoulder, and explained something very important to him.

'Sergei, everything and anyone I touch, I only do it for humanity's good. These houses are for poor old people who have no place to live properly. And if I tried to explain to you how I built them in one day, you would not believe me.'

'Problem is, Rabbi Mordechai, is that after what happened with my wife, I would believe you... I don't know what to do,' said Sergei.

'You know that sometimes my methods cannot be explained. Remember when your daughter Irina was having trouble getting into the University?

Remember how I transferred the money and got her registered from a distance, and when she got back to the University the next day the secretary was amazed to see that all was written properly in her log and Irina was a registered student who had paid her bills, overnight?

So I say, don't ask questions, Sergei. What does it matter? The houses are here now. But you have no reason to worry. If needed, I can make the houses disappear. Close your eyes for just a minute.'

Sergei closed his eyes, and I restored the blanket. 'Open them now, Sergei.' He did, and practically jumped, so surprised he was.

The houses were not there. The two policemen were so scared by this phenomenon that they dropped their guns and ran away. Sergei stepped over and picked up the guns, automatically, staring at the direction of the houses that were not there.

'The fools,' he said, almost to himself. 'They probably think it's the Devil's work... But Rabbi Mordechai, all your work! Making it disappear like that. How? Why?'

'I can bring them back,' I said. 'If you close your eyes again, I will do so.' He did, and the houses returned. Sergei was shaken.

'You are playing with my head, Rabbi Mordechai. Are you trying to scare me?' said Sergei. 'I know you are not the Devil, but honestly... So you can make them disappear and appear at will? Won't it be dangerous to the people inside?'

'No, I can get them out first,' I said.

'But what if my supervisors hear about it and come to inspect?'

'You will give me warning, and I'll make the houses disappear.'

'Ah, well,' said Sergei, giving up. 'I'll close my eyes to the whole thing and tell my policemen that if they don't shut up the Devil will get them.'"

"What a story," I said. "And did any trouble follow these events"

"No. Strangely enough, nothing ever happened to disturb the people I moved into these houses. Somehow, the police never talked, and the occupants were safe. Of course, such houses, built by supernatural phenomena, are not permanent. They last ten, fifteen years, no more.
But when they disappear, I will find another solution. Anyway, Germain, I have other, very important things to tell you. Are you beginning to realize who and what I am?"

"I suspect you are an Ulema, Rabbi Mordechai, as well as an alchemist and a Kabbalist. Too much coincidence if you are not Ulema..."

Rabbi Mordechai laughed loudly and clapped his hands. "What a boy. He is not stupid, after all..."

*** *** ***

Here are some fabulous stories told by Germain Lumiere who is now visiting Ulema Mordechai in Budapest, Hungary.

Germain Lumiere said, verbatim:
Budapest is an interesting city in its design, since it is really comprised of two separate entities. The River Danube flows into the city from north to south. Buda, the residential area, is situated on the hills to the West. Pest, the commercial area, is located on a flat plain. Rabbi Mordechai's house was located in a quiet street in Buda.
It was a typically large, three storied, Eastern European stone house, with low windows secured with metal bars. Inside, the place was simply and comfortably furnished, and my room, where he took me to put down the suitcase, was indeed spacious and pleasant.
A charming rounded wood burning stove was standing there, though being summer, it was not lit. A large, old fashioned dark wood armoire, beautifully carved, probably 18th Century, a bed piled with pillows and standing under the window, and a desk with a chair, completed the furniture.
The window overlooked a big, lush garden.
I expected Rabbi Mordechai to have a lab, perhaps with a machine that could transmute drawings into gold, like the one he had in Mr. Markowitch's house in Paris, but he did not have either. His work, apparently, was done in the library, a large room lined with books on all sides. It had a couple of big wooden tables heaped with more books, papers, and writing implements, and several comfortable old armchairs for reading.
He left me there, and went to get us coffee and lunch. I suspected, quite correctly, that during my stay in Budapest I would be spending most of my time in that room, so I started to walk around, checked the eclectic collection of books of so many subjects that they would make an ordinary person's head spin, and admired a large and handsome old globe that stood on one of the tables.
I always liked globes, so I gave this one a twirl with my finger, and watched it spin.

"Which country did you hit on with your finger?" asked Rabbi Mordechai, entering the room with a tray just as I was doing it.

"I have no idea," I said, surprised. Does it matter? I was just playing..."

Rabbi Mordechai looked at me with a mysterious air. "Yes, sometimes it does," he said, smiling benevolently at me. "We are going to do some interesting things with this globe. Come, eat, you must be starving after the long trip!" I had no objection and came to the table. Rabbi Mordechai swept aside a stack of papers, put a few books on the floor, and poured me a cup of excellent Turkish coffee.

The light meal was very tasty, with delicious olives from Klamata, which, he told me, were given to him by an old Greek gentleman as a token of friendship, good bread, and a white, spicy cheese, made into small balls that floated in olive oil. The cheese, he said, was brought by another friend, an old woman from Albania. "Yes," he said.

"These are good, old-fashioned people, they show their love by bringing such nice gifts, how could I refuse? I do my best for them in return. It's the way people used to live in villages, in the old days, helping each other, bringing gifts..."

"I imagine you do a lot more for them than they do for you, Rabbi Mordechai, knowing your record of helping people. But still, it's nice, you don't have to do a lot of shopping," I said. "And it's very kind of them."

"Yes, what do I need? As you know, I am a vegetarian just like you and your family, and I never touch meat or fish. All I need, after I get such delicacies as gifts, is bread, rice, and beans, since I grow all the fruit and vegetables I eat in my garden. For me, the simple life is best." It was an interesting comment, since I knew he could live like a Sultan from the Arabian Nights tales if he so wished, being able to manufacture gold at will.

But the Ulema view luxury as childish toys, and only indulge in it if there is a need or a cause that demands it. However, as for the food, it turned out he was a superb cook. With simple ingredients and a kitchen that did not have elaborate and fancy tools, he could create meals that would be fit for royalty.

I learned a lot of cooking from him and valued the skill very much over the years, particularly when I could later surprise guests who thought vegetarian eating was dull, by presenting them with a vegetarian banquet, cooked by myself, that would amaze them with its variety, colors and delicate taste and style.

When we finished the meal, I helped him stack the dishes on the tray, and asked, "Where is the kitchen? I'll go and wash up."

"I'd better show you," he said. We went into the living room, and in the far side of it was a heavy wooden door. "Watch out, there are three stairs here," he said, as he opened the door. The kitchen, at this lower level, was quite large, but extremely primitive. I wanted to put the olive jar and the cheese in the refrigerator, but as I looked around for it, I did not see one.

"Where is the refrigerator?" I asked.

"I don't have one," he said.

"So where do you store the food?" I asked, surprised, still holding the tray and not knowing where to put it.

"On this table," he said. I looked, and saw a table piled with vegetables, more cheese, bread, and many other foodstuffs. "But doesn't the food spoil much quicker, without a refrigerator? If they are not available here, can't people get iceboxes, at least?"

"Well, yes, many people do," said Rabbi Mordechai, smiling at some funny idea of his own that I did not understand, "but I don't need one. Take a look at these things, they are much better." He pointed to three small objects that stood on the table around the food. They were made of crystal, and shaped like pyramids. I had no idea what purpose they served.

"Let me show you. Put the tray on the chair next to the table, then take the olive and cheese jars and put them somewhere between these triangles," he said. I assumed that by saying "triangles" he meant the crystal pyramids, so just as he said, I went to the table, put the tray on the chair, and placed the jars at the center of the table, between the pyramids.

I was startled by the sensation of extreme cold that enveloped my hands and arms as I placed the jars on the table. The atmosphere in the room was comfortably warm.

The atmosphere between the crystal pyramids was icy cold, as cold as a freezer. Rabbi Mordechai laughed aloud and beat the arm of the chair, making the dishes rattle alarmingly. "There are other options than technology," he said. "The triangles keep the food fresh much longer..."

"You are playing tricks again!" I accused him, jokingly.

"Why not?" he said, smiling. "Knowledge does not have to take away your sense of humor, son! Life is fun!"

Indeed life with Rabbi Mordechai was always fun, even though we studied very hard, every day, all day long. My only complaint was that sometimes he would be argumentative and use semantics that did not make sense to me, but the work itself was so interesting and engaging that it did not matter. Also, I felt that some of the techniques he demonstrated to me were simply tricks used to show off, though now I realize how wrong I was. Well, I was young, I suppose, and naturally there was much I could not understand. Around six o'clock we usually had our dinner, then went out for a walk, and he showed me a lot of the beautiful sights of Budapest.

Time passed quickly.

I have learned so much, everything of which, Rabbi Mordechai promised, would enable me to succeed in my meeting with the Pères du Triangle, and later in all my endeavors in life. But something, I knew, was still missing, and I was very hesitant asking about it. One day I gathered all my courage and asked him, "What about the opening of the Conduit?"

"It will happen soon enough," he said.

"But is there work to be done in preparation? What is the process?"

"It varies," said Rabbi Mordechai. "Come on, let's go out, you are tired from so much study." I certainly was, since that evening we continued working after our dinner, having been engaged in an interesting study, so we did not go to our usual walk. It was rather late at night, and I felt I would enjoy a little fresh air. "Let's go to one of the bridges between Buda and Pest," said Rabbi Mordechai. "It's a pleasant night for a walk."

"Which one should we go to?" I asked.

"Let's go to the Széchenyi Lánchíd, the Chain Bridge," said Rabbi Mordechai. I certainly had no objection to that; this bridge was a thing of beauty. It was called after Count Istvan Széchenyi, who had commissioned it, and was the first of the eight permanent bridges in the city. The Count invested much thought and effort in building the bridge.

He not only asked a French authority, Marc Isambard Brunel, for advice, but even went to examine William Tierney Clark's bridge across the Thames at Marlow, England, before finalizing his plans. The bridge was built between 1839 and 1849, and the stunning lions at each end were designed by the great sculptor, János Marschalko.

There is a great debate regarding the lions' tongues. Some say that they are there, though extremely hard to find even if you climb all the way up the pedestals on the four corners of the bridge.

Others say there are no tongues at all, and tell a legend that during the opening ceremony, a little boy noticed that the tongues were not there, and told the sculptor. Poor Marschalko was so distraught by realizing he had forgotten such an important detail, that he hurled himself off the bridge to his death.

It was late at night, there was no one present on the bridge, and the lights of the city reflected beautifully in the dark water. We stood for a moment, enjoying the sight, and then Rabbi Mordechai said, quite suddenly, "How long do you think it will take you to cross the bridge?"

"I don't know," I said, trying to estimate the length.
"Would you like to bet I can do it quicker than you?" he asked, his blue green eyes twinkling with amusement.

"Sure," I said, laughing. "Why not?"

"Good," he said. "But you must walk straight and not look back or even to the sides." I knew he had something up his sleeve, but it was fun to play the game. "Very well," I said. "Shall I start?"

"Go!" he said, laughing, and I started walking, looking ahead, avoiding looking back or to the sides. When I reached the end of the bridge, Rabbi Mordechai was standing there, leaning against it, smiling.

"I see," I said. "Very impressive. I would like to learn this technique."

"I am happy to hear that you are not calling it a trick," said Rabbi Mordechai, seriously.

"No, I don't think this is a trick," I said. I felt a vague regret. Have I let Rabbi Mordechai down by being skeptical? Were there some subtle points I have missed?

"Let's go to the other side," he said. "Would you like to try how this technique feels?"

"Yes, I would," I said. In a fraction of a second, I was on the other side of the bridge, without any delay or even any sensation. I was just there, while a second ago, I was elsewhere.

Rabbi Mordechai was not near me. I looked at the bridge, and I saw him walking toward me.

Obviously, he wanted to show me that I was not hallucinating. If we were both transported together, I might have suspected that we never really left and it was only some sort of hallucination, another trick, but seeing Rabbi Mordechai walking on the bridge would prevent any such suspicion. He wanted to reassure me, as I thought. I had shown a sad lack of trust, and perhaps I had hurt this great, forgiving, loving friend who would do anything for me. How could I? I felt so ashamed.

When he came to the other side, I said, "Rabbi Mordechai, I know why you transported me and walked yourself. I understand your motive. But it is no longer necessary to do so. I fully trust you. I am your student, forever."

Rabbi Mordechai looked at me with tears in his eyes, and hugged me with all his might. "You are more than my student, Germain. You are my son from now on." A great wave of happiness and peace flowed through me. He was not angry, he understood, he knew I placed all my trust in him and I was forgiven...

Suddenly, I felt something I could not explain, something that happened in my mind, or in my brain, or in my soul, something that I could not prove but was as tangible as the river and the houses. The ability to trust I have so suddenly discovered in myself burst open the gates in my mind, and my Conduit opened.

I staggered a little, caught on to the bridge, and recovered almost instantly. The world felt different than before, but I was still myself.

"How did it happen so fast?" I asked.

"It was not fast at all," said Rabbi Mordechai. "It was exactly as it should be, as it always is, and always will be. You see, your other masters taught you many things, and there was an enormous amount of dormant knowledge which was accumulated in your mind and constantly fed by them.
And now, at the right time, and under the right circumstances, and encouraged by your ability to accept the Ulema way, the Conduit opened, by itself, like a flower. You are now ready to start on the road to being full- fledged Ulema. Welcome, my son."

Note: In addition to all those beautiful and extraordinary "things" an Anunnaki-Ulema can do, here is a synopsis of some of their most intriguing and fabulous capabilities:
1. Learning a new language in less than two hours.
2. Seeing very clearly in the dark.
3. Controlling the heart rhythm/speed.
4. Reading others' thoughts.
5. Seeing others' aura.
6. Stopping external bleeding instantly.
7. Seeing a certain number of future events. (Not predicting!)
8. Fully controlling physical pain.
9. Looking young (approximately 37) permanently. Stopping the physical appearances of aging.
10. Sensing and understanding bad and good vibes, and how to block the effects of negative vibes.
11. Moving objects at distance.
12. Teleportation.
13. Traversing solid objects, such as walls.
14. Finishing multiple tasks fifty times faster than others.
15. Recovering from injuries in an amazing speed.
16. Influencing others in decision making, though only for a good purpose.
17. Controlling electrical and electronic supplies and gadgets
18. Reading a big book in minutes.
19. Acquiring the healing touch.
20. Communicating through telepathy (sending and receiving messages).
21. Entering and exiting parallel dimensions.
22. Communicating with the Double.
23. Communicating with a deceased person during the 40 days period following his/her death.
24. Communicating with animals.
25. Partially changing the molecular properties of objects and substances.

*** *** ***

48. Brain "The Supersymetric Mind"
⌘⌘⌘

Study of the influence of the Anunnaki's programming of our brain and fate.

- I. Introduction
- II. Excerpts from Ulema Sorenztein's Kira'at
- III. The Supersymetric Mind
- a. A brief note on supersymetry
- b. What is a "Supersymetric Mind"?

48. Brain "The Supersymetric Mind"
⌘⌘⌘

Study of the influence of the Anunnaki's programming of our brain and fate.

- I. Introduction
- II. Excerpts from Ulema Sorenztein's Kira'at
- III. The Supersymetric Mind
- a. A brief note on supersymetry
- b. What is a "Supersymetric Mind"?

I. Introduction:
Honorable Ulema Sorenstein once said, "...in many cases, some people are responsible for their own bad luck and failure in life. It all depends on what you put in your Araya/Conduit brain zones."
He added: "Even though, the human mind was created the way the Anunnaki wanted it, and even though, your brain had been programmed and fashioned 65,000 years ago, and "upgraded" and reconditioned by the Anunnaki some 6,000 to 7,000 years ago, you can still bring important changes to your mind, and make it work for you like a charm."

He continued:
"Everything depends on:

- 1-How to store your ideas and thoughts in your brain;
- 2-Which idea, thought, or vision will you consciously allow to enter your brain;
- 3-How to control the vibrations of your ideas, visions, and thoughts;

- 4-How to scan your ideas, visions, and thoughts that are stored on the Araya net;
- 5-How to stabilize the vibrations of your mind;
- 6-How to get rid of bad thoughts and symptoms of a "weak personality" that prevent you from succeeding in life and getting a good job;
- 7-How to prevent the vibrations of a bad thought from deteriorating or "killing" the vibrations of good thoughts, etc...
- And something else you should remember, you are not the slave of the genetic creation of the Anunnaki who created all of us."

Note: Ulema Sorenstein is a modern American Ulema, originally from Latvia. He lived in Lower Manhattan area in New York City, and he is 135 year old. You look at him, and you don't give him more than 37.
Many people have seen him in different places, simultaneously. We will comment later on what he meant by:
a-"Responsible for their own bad luck and failure",
b- "Araya/Conduit";
c- "Brain zones".
But first, let's listen to his Anunnaki-Ulema Kira'at on success and failure in life, and in business.

*** *** ***

II. Excerpts from Ulema Sorenstein's Kira'at, as provided by Ulema Maximillien de Lafayette
(As is, and unedited):

- Many of you came to me and asked me why some people are luckier than others?
- Or why Elizabeth is making more money than Patricia?
- Or why this person is more successful than another person, knowing well that he is a spiritual and a good man, and also very intelligent, while the other person is less spiritual and not so bright?
- Does intelligence or morality has anything to do with success in life, and/or the way our brain was wired by the Anunnaki, at the time they created us?

- My answer to you is this: Intelligence is very important but does not always guarantee success in life. Many great inventors died penniless.
- Morality is very important in life, but many spiritual people were murdered because of their moral principles.
- Morality and intelligence have nothing to do with your success in life (Your life on this Earth.)
- The high standard of morality and intelligence of a person does not change luck, decrease or increase your luck and success in your life.
- I guess, you are concerned with social success, financial success, or something like that. Well, let's talk about your financial success and success in your career.
- I will take an example from your modern city, from your modern life, from your modern society where you live, so you will understand me perfectly.
- In 1989, Melissa, Peggy, and Esther graduated from NYU with a doctorate degree in education. They have identical credentials, and three of them are of the same age. They are healthy, and intelligent, and want to succeed in life.
- Usually, when you are not an entrepreneur, you look for a job. Melissa, Peggy, and Esther are not entrepreneurs. Their greatest asset is their academic advanced degree. Very good.
- In the modern world of science, education, technology, and knowledge, education is extremely important, and a degree should help a lot.
- A few years later, let's say 1999 for example, you learned that Melissa became the Secretary of Education; Peggy is a high school teacher in San Diego; and Esther is working as a telemarketer in Brooklyn.
- Now, we start to wonder, how come Melissa got a very prestigious and a high profile job in Washington, while Peggy and Esther did not?
- After all, if credentials are required, all of them have the same qualifications and same credentials. So what is going on here?
- Why Peggy is working as a school teacher, and not as a superintendent or director of the school in San Diego, or as an education commissioner?

- And why Esther is working as a telemarketer getting $10 or $15 an hour?
- What did happen to these three highly educated and lovely ladies?
- Image makers, public relations advisors, headhunters, human resources directors, and even psychologists will avalanche you with all sorts of reasons, ranging from personality, contact, luck, political or social affiliations, ambition, job search strategies, networking, location, and even because the way a resume was written.
- All these reasons and explanations have some merits. But they do not explain why Esther could not get a better job, or at least a better pay, taking into consideration the doctorate degree she has earned. After all, such a high academic degree requires a sound and developed mind, knowledge, determination, perseverance, and analytical approach to things in life. All these qualities should have served and helped Esther in finding a better job.
- Well, the Ulema have a different explanation.
- Although, the Ulema recognize the validity, practicality, and importance of the explanations given by those experts in the field, the Ulema believe that what you call "Luck", success and prosperity are already fashioned, and written on the front page of the book of your life.
- What was already decided upon vis-à-vis your success in life can be found (And sometime changed and totally transformed by your own will) in the Araya Zones of your brain. A brain that was genetically created by the Anunnaki. And I am going to explain to you what I mean by Araya, brain's zone, Conduit's activation, and your genetic brain.
- Now, you have to remember that everything in the world emits vibrations.
- And all sorts of vibrations occupy a place in the world.
- Some vibrations are detectable, some are not.
- Some vibrations, modern science recognizes, detects, and registers, and some are not yet known to science and mental health empiric efforts.
- The same thing is happening right now in your brain.
- The word "world" means everything that surrounds you, including distant planets, galaxies and extra-dimensions.

- The "world" also means the infinitesimal zones in the Araya which is in your brain.
- The Araya is the domain, the realm, the landscape where 73 different zones of your brain are found.
- Each zone of the Araya functions differently, because it was created, engineered and programmed differently by the Anunnaki, at the time the prototypes and final "models" of the human race were created.
- And yes, the $10 per hour Esther is getting as a telemarketer in Brooklyn has a lot to do with the Araya, and one region of her Araya.
- I am getting there. Be very patient with me. If you are not patient and you rush to a speedy answer, you will miss the boat, and you will become very confused.
- At the end of the Kira'at, everything will become clear to you.
- Now, let's go back to the vibrations.
- Every thought, each idea you have in your brain, has a vibration. And each vibration occupies a spot in your Araya, called "Jaba".
- Let's simply things and call Araya now a net.
- This net has many holes, called "Jabas".
- Each Jaba (A hole, so to speak) stores one idea.
- And each idea or thought in the Jaba of the net produces a vibration.
- For example, if the net has 70,000 Jabas, your brain will be able to store 70,000 ideas and thoughts.
- This means, that your Araya hosts 70,000 vibrations. And that is full capacity.
- Some people who are more creative than you could have 300,000 ideas and thoughts stored in 300,000 Jabas (Holes or locations) in your Araya (Net).
- The good thoughts and good ideas in your Araya do not expand. They stay well balanced and well synchronized where they are (Inside the Jaba of the net).
- There, they are safe and protected.
- Only bad thoughts, and bad ideas, such as fear, low self-esteem, stubbornness, hate, indecisiveness, laziness, tendency toward violence, badmouthing people, envy, jealousy, betrayal, so on, emit vibrations that overflow

- the perimeter (Circumference) of the Jaba (Hole or location) that stores your thought or idea.
- This phenomenon (Overflow) takes over the adjacent Jaba(s) containing a good idea or a good thought.
- Because the negative energy inside your mind is usually stronger than the positive energy of a good thought, the Jaba on the net (Location) containing a good thought or a good idea shrinks, gets contaminated, and stops to emit positive and creative energy.
- This, kills the good thoughts and good ideas in your Araya.
- If this continues, all good and creative ideas and thoughts in your brain will be damaged and neutralized by your bad thoughts and ideas. In other words, many cells in your brain's or Araya's, and their creative mental faculties stored in the Jaba become dysfunctional; atrophied or dead.
- In this case, you are responsible for causing this deterioration. Nobody has forced you to think about bad thoughts or bad ideas. It is your own doing.
- You might say, I have no control over all this.
- Things happen. Ideas come and go.
- And I will tell you, you are wrong, because you can control your ideas and your thoughts, and make them work for you in a very healthy, positive and productive way.
- I will explain to you how you can do that very shortly.
- The most destructive thoughts that prevent you from succeeding in life are:
- a-Low self-esteem;
- b-Fear (Fear of anything);
- c-Unwillingness to accept new ideas;
- d-Bitterness;
- e-Constantly contradicting others because you have developed a complex of inferiority, and not because of a complex of superiority;
- f-Negativity.

Note: a to f are not categorically part of the Anunnaki's primordial (Original) makeup of the genetic creation of your mind. Your upbringing, way or life, and personal vision of the world and your immediate environment could have caused this.

- Let's go back to Esther' situation, and see whether the Anunnaki are responsible for a lack of a great success in her life, considering the very advanced academic degree she earned, or whether Esther's own actions, thoughts, personality, or her bad "luck" prevented her from getting a better job.
- And above all, let's see what the Ulema recommend.
- In life, we have to simplify things to understand them. So, let's approach Esther's situation in a very simple manner.
- It is more likely that a, b, d, and f, have created the unpleasant condition of Esther.
- The symptoms a, b, d, and f, emanate negative and destructive vibrations in the Araya, causing the Jaba(s) to shrink.
- And when the Jaba(s) shrink, the human being ceased to become creative and resourceful.
- The vibrations of a, b, d, and f overflow the Jaba. And you already know what happens when the overflow occurs and invades other Jabas.
- The lack of creative thinking and resourcefulness blended with negativity and low self-esteem will prevent any person from getting the kind of job or occupation, she/he deserved.
- And this is exactly what happened to Esther.
- In the Jaba(s), the Anunnaki have installed and implanted sequences of ideas, thoughts and faculties that shape the future and the "human cosmography" of all humans.
- The symptoms a, b, d, and f, were never the primordial ingredients of the Araya or the Jaba.
- This is very good, because it shows that the human race is not enslaved by the genetic makeup/design of the human race, by the Anunnaki.
- Many writers, and conspiracy theories advocates in the Western hemisphere, and particularly in the United States, so erroneously have claimed that the

Anunnaki are controlling the world; the Anunnaki are our masters; the human race is enslaved by the Anunnaki; the governments of the world are controlled by the Anunnaki. This is untrue.
- But what is true is that the brain as designed by the Anunnaki cannot escape or go beyond the genetic specifications of the Anunnaki.
- However, the Anunnaki have no absolute control over our brain, (Araya, and Jabas), since they have allowed us to activate the "Conduit" in our brain.
- And since all of us have more than one "single brain", wonderful things can be accomplished, and our freedom will always be protected.
- The Ulema believe that the human brain is in fact a "Supersymetric Brain".
- And I will explain this to you.
- Because once you fully understand how your "Supersymetric Brain" functions, you will be able to make miracles, and heal yourself from many things.
- But you should never ever claim, that the Anunnaki-Ulema's healing and therapy methods do replace or substitute for any traditional, and scientific means and methods of treatment, and diagnosis, as applied in traditional medicine, and/or in other legitimate mental health practices.

*** *** ***

III. The "Supersymetric Mind": "Ma bira-rach" Excerpts from Ulema Sorenstein's Kira'at, as is, and unedited.

a. A brief note on supersymetry:

> According to the theory of supersymetry, also known as SUSY, all particles in the known universe have their counter-part, also called super-partner(s).
> Basically, this is the view of quantum physics scientists and theorists. In the Anunnaki-Ulema context, supersymetry is either the similar or the opposite of YOU.
> In a limited sense, it is the other super-partner of "you", and what constitutes you at all levels; organically, bio-organically, chemically, genetically, etherically, atomically, mentally and physically.
> The most important and predominant part of your mind-body supersymetry is your mind. Because everything starts in your mind. In this context, your mind is a "Supersymetric Mind".

b. What is a "Supersymetric Mind"?

- You were brought up to believe that every person in the world has a brain; one single brain.
- Nobody seems to contradict this. And I do not contradict this either.
- However, this "single brain" is not the only brain you have, at least in this dimension.
- All of us, enlightened or not have two brains; the first brain is the one we are aware of, and familiar with, from studying anatomy, medicine and other disciplines, and the other mind, is the one that co-existed, and currently co-exists side-by-side your brain, and outside your body.
- It is called the supersymetric mind. In Ana'kh, it is called "Ma bira-rach".

- For now, let's compare Ma bira-rach to your "Double".
- As you already know, the Double means the etheric image of your physical body.
- Ma bira-rach is the etheric image of your brains. But we call it supersymetric, because the particles constituting the physical and etheric mind can de detected and scanned scientifically.
- In the Western hemisphere, and particularly in the United States, the theory of supersymetry has received a warm welcome in the scientific community.
- Scanning the physical brain has become a scientific reality. But scanning the etheric brain has never been done in the West.
- The Anunnaki-Ulema (Mounawariin) know how to scan both the physical and etheric substance of your brains. And I have to remind you here, that you should never ever attempt to scan your mind or others' mind using any means or methods that constitute and illegal medical practice. Leave it to physicians, medical technicians, and those who are authorized by the law to do so.
- Two methods have been used by the Anunnaki-Ulema. To scan the brains (Mind). One is purely scientific; the other is metascientific, which is totally incomprehensible and unrealistic to Western scientists.
- The Anunnaki-Ulema's scientific method consists of implanting on the "surface of the tissues" of your brains mobile microscopic devices that move around and scan the Jaba(s) of you brains.
- The devices detect tumors, deterioration of the cells, and repair the damaged cells.
- In the United States, some have compared these devices to the very small metallic objects, an extraterrestrial race (Greys) has implanted inside the bodies of abductees. This is totally incorrect.
- According to some legitimate physicians (involved with some sort of ufology in the United States,) who have treated those abductees, these devices are of an "alien substance and origin". The main function of these alien devices is to monitor the abductees, and to serve as "receiver-emitter" of aliens' messages.
- I will not comment on their claims.

- But one thing I will tell you for sure: The Anunnaki-Ulema implants are not tracking devices. Because once, the cell damages are repaired, the implants disintegrate, lose their mass, and the human body flushed them out, the normal way.
- The Anunnaki-Ulema scientific mind (Brains) scanning occurs in that manner. The scanning is a physical and a real operation.
- This idea might seem strange and absurd to many scientists in the West.
- However, we have learned that many military scientists, psychiatrists, and surgeons, in the West are exploring these techniques.
- My prediction is that in the very near future, the United States of America will be using these devices implants techniques in hospitals and medical facilities.
- As to the second Anunnaki-Ulema etheric mind scanning techniques, well, these techniques are taught to our students, and do not require a surgical operation.
- You can scan the mind, and bring comfort to your mind and your body by either activating the Conduit or superposing the Araya (Net of the mind) of your physical mind and the Araya of your supersymetric mind (Your other mind that exists as a bulk of separate particles in an etheric substance.)
- Using this second technique, you will be able to neutralize the vibrations of the cells storing bad thoughts and bad ideas, such as bitterness, negativity, lack of energy, laziness, indecisiveness, and fear.
- This second technique is called "Ma bi-idawa".
- I will explain Ma bi idawa in my next Kira'at.

Notes:
- **1**-Ma bi idawa is outlined and explained in book 4 of this series "The Anunnaki Ulema Final Warning: Humanity destiny, UFOs threat, and the extraterrestrials final solution", and in book 6 "Anunnaki Self Healing."
- **2**-The Anunnaki-Ulema scientific mind (Brains) scanning via devices implants in the human body is not science fiction literature.

Allegedly, surgeons and psychiatrists who worked on the CIA Mind Control Program in the fifties, sixties, and early seventies have attempted to develop and implement quasi-similar techniques on volunteers, and retarded patients.

- 3-Most recently, a vast literature and avalanches of scientific papers on this subject appear in the American scientific community, and many physicians, scientists, and futurists advanced mind-boggling theories on these implants techniques, on a theoretical level.

Nevertheless, what was theory in the past is nowadays a pragmatic application and standard procedures in many scientific fields.

Dean Takahashi stated that "Nanorobotics (Known also as the Nanotechnology Robots) is a hypothetical concept.

Basic nanomachines are already in use. Nanobots will be the next generation of nanomachines.

Advanced nanobots will be able to sense and adapt to environmental stimuli such as heat, light, sounds, surface textures, and chemicals; perform complex calculations; move, communicate, and work together; conduct molecular assembly; and, to some extent, repair or even replicate themselves.

Nanotechnology is the science and application of creating objects on a level smaller than 100 nanometers. The extreme concept of nanotechnology is the "bottom up" creation of virtually any material or object by assembling one atom at a time.

Although nanotech processes occur at the scale of nanometers, the materials and objects that result from these processes can be much larger.

Large-scale results happen when nanotechnology involves massive parallelism in which many simultaneous and synergistic nanoscale processes combine to produce a large-scale result."

*** *** ***

49. The Duplicate Image or Reproduction of a Being "Ishra"
⌘ ⌘ ⌘

I. Definition
II. Ulema Mordechai ben Zvi explains

I. Definition:
Ishra is the name or term for the new image or duplicate of the original existence of a life-form, in another universe.

II. Ulema Mordechai ben Zvi explains:
Anunnaki-Ulema Modechai ben Zvi said:
"All living forms, including humans and animals have many duplicates of themselves throughout the universe.
In each dimension, physical and non-physical, we find identical, symmetrical and alive copy of all of us. This copy is not a visual reproduction or a holographic projection, but real in every single detail. This could be explained by the fact that multiple universes are "so created". And this creation which goes on ad infinitum encompasses anything and everything that exists and/or has exited anywhere. Each time, a new universe is created, whether it is parallel or in another dimension, the creation process includes every single molecule that has created a previous universe, or has been a part of it."

*** *** ***

50. Apparition of Dead Pets. Communication with our Dead Pets "Gensi-uzuru"
⌘ ⌘ ⌘

I. Introduction
II. Is it possible to communicate with our dead pets?
III. When your departed loved pet returns to see you
IV. Excerpts from Master Li's Kira'at on Gensi-uzuru

I. Introduction:
The Ulema are very fond of animals. Extensive passages in the Book of Rama-Dosh speak about the important role animals play in the life of humans, especially at emotional and therapeutic levels. The Ulema believe that pets understand very well their human-friends (Instead of using the word "owners"). And also, pets communicate with those who show them love and affection. This loving relationship between pets and their human-friends does not end when pets die.

II. Is it possible to communicate with our dead pets?
Although the Anunnaki-Ulema do not believe in any possibility of contacting deceased people or animals, they have explained to us that contacting our departed ones is possible for a very short time, and only during the 40 days period following their death.
In other words, we can contact our deceased parents and dear ones, or more accurately enter in contact with them if:

- **a-**They contact us short after their death;
- **b-**They must initiate the contact;
- **c-**This should happen during a 40 days period following their departure;
- **d-**Their contact (Physical or non-physical) must be noticed by us. This means that we should and must pay an extra attention to "something" quite irregular or

unusual happening around us. Because our departed pets will try to send us messages, and in many instances, they do.
- **e**-We must expect their messages, and strongly believe in those messages.

The Ulema said that humans cannot contact their dead pets. But pets can contact us via different ways, that we can sense if we have developed a strong bond with them. Pets know who love them and those who don't, because pets feel, understand, sense and see our aura. All our feelings and thoughts are imprinted in our aura, and the aura is easily visible to pets, particularly, cats, dogs, parrots, lionesses, pigs, and horses.

This belief is shared by authors, people of science and therapists in the West, despite major difference between Westerners and Ulema in defining the nature and limits of pets-humans after death contact.

For instance, in the United States, pets lovers and several groups of therapists and psychics think that "a pet can reappear as a ghost, and a ghost could be luminous or even appear as it did in life. You don't necessarily know when you see an animal if it's a ghost or not, said Warren, a researcher in the field. "It's much easier to identify a loved one who's passed and come back."

"Don't forget them because they're gone," said Jungles, who owns three cats. "Keep their toys and blankets around.

They (ghosts) will go where they're happiest." Warren agrees. "Recreate an environment conducive to the pet's life," he said. "Use your imagination and treat it like it's alive. In other words, you should create or re-create conditions ideal for their re-appearance, even though, for a very short moment.

III. When your departed loved pet returns to see you:
I remember very vividly what the loving and Honorable Ulema Li has said to a novice who rushed to him in tears, and begged him to bring back to life, his dog who had died that morning.

This happened some sixty years ago. Here is the story.

My loving teacher asked the little Murad (Name of the novice): When did your dog die?

Murad: This morning Master, please bring him back to me!

Master Li: I can't do that son, but how about if I let you see him one more time?

Murad: Oh Master, I will do anything for you, anything.

Master Li: You know son, you dog is not dead. He is somewhere else now and he is very happy.
Murad: Master, I buried him this morning under the tree. He is dead, he is dead!
Master Li: Ok then, l will let you see him one more time, but do not touch him, do you understand? Just look at him, you can talk to him, but do not touch him. If you touch him, Poof, he will disappear.
Note: By then, many students were alerted to what was going on and rushed to sit on the floor at the feet of the Master, excited and curious, they kept looking at the Master and I could hear them saying Master, please one more miracle, because they were accustomed to see the Master doing extraordinary things. An indescribable deep silence threw its heavy coat over the little students... and we were waiting...
And all of a sudden, Murad screamed: Ahhhh...he is scratching my legs...he is licking my right foot...he is here...I feel him...Where is Master? Where is he, please tell me...I want to see him.
None of the students −including myself− saw or felt anything. Only Murad. Then, a thin layer of white dust began to take shape. And suddenly the dust was transformed into a substance like fluffy white cotton, and finally the face of a small dog began to appear, and seconds later, his whole body became visible to all of us. Murad got so excited and so happy...and not remembering what the Master has told him, rushed to hug his dog. And this was a grave mistake. Because as soon as he touched the face of his dog, the dog vanished in thin air. What Murad did upset everybody, and we hated him for that!
Obviously Murad is in state of shock now. He did not know what to do or what to say. He dropped on the ground, and almost fell in a coma. The dog never returned again.
With an austere serenity, the Master was watching everything, and everybody. Then, almost in a perfect synchronization, the students shouted: Master! What happened? And very calmly, the Master said: "You never touch the body of the dead before he rises to a higher dimension." None of us understood what he meant. We kept on asking more and more questions, but the Master in a firm voice said: "The Dirasa did not start yet!" (Dirasa means the lesson or the study.)
Two months later, the Master nicely surprised us with a lesson on Gensi-uzuru. Obviously, he did not forget how interested we

were in learning more about what has happened to Murad's dog. Everybody was excited beyond belief. And this is what the Master had to say:

IV. Excerpts from Master Li's Kira'at on Gensi-uzuru:

- The Anunnaki love their pets very much. They treat them with love and respect. They do not consider them animals, but friends who just look different.
- You too, all of you, should love and care for you pets.
- Your pets feel with you, and know if you love them or you don't.
- Your pets can even protect your health and some other time, I will tell you more about it.
- When your pets die, they don't forget you. Like all of us, they remember their good friends.
- And believe me when I tell you, they will try to come back, because they want so much to be with you again. Unfortunately, this is not possible.
- However, and because of the great love you had for your pets, they will keep on trying and trying.
- Pets are like humans...after they die, they don't understand what is happening to them. They become very confused.
- But this happens to your pets during two weeks only. The two weeks after they have died. After these two weeks, their essence is no longer trapped in the thin sphere separating Earth (More exactly, previous life) from the next dimension. So after two weeks, they are gone for good.
- For humans, it is 40 days. After 40 days, we are no longer here. We enter the next dimension, and we never come back.
- So, during these two weeks (Two weeks after they die), your pets can return to see you for a very very short moment. It could last up to 4 seconds.
- Now, it is up to you to feel their presence. It is not difficult if you pay attention.
- I am going to explain to you.

- First, what they do is this: Because they are no longer in a physical substance,(Physical form), and because they don't know what is happening them, they approach you very slowly. They are confused, but they recognize you.
- They still remember where they were before.
- They remember your home, you, and the toys they played with; the ones you gave them.
- So, they come toward you slowly slowly, and gently will lean against your legs, or touch your legs like a whisper, like a child's caress.
- Unfortunately, very very very few people notice that. And sadly enough, your pets' desperate efforts to contact you and let you know that they here around you are almost never felt.
- So, they dissipate, because they run out of energy.
- Remember, they can't last for more than 4 seconds.
- But they don't give up. They will try one more time. Only one more time. After that, they are gone for ever.
- Now listen to me carefully. While you are not aware of their invisible existence around you, things are still happening, and you can be part of it.
- You can still make some small arrangements, and mentally and emotionally prepare yourself to feel them when they return. And you will succeed. So what you have to do is this:
- Go fetch their toys. All of them if possible. Put them in their favorite area, where they used to play with their toys or preferred to lay down.
- Sit on the floor around the toys. Remember, you can't call your dead pets. You can't communicate with them. But they will communicate with you and will return to see you for the last time.
- Bring their food and water bowls, and put them next to their toys, as if they were still alive. Don't ask why, just do it.
- Stay there for sometime. Twenty minutes should suffice. You can leave the room, but it is imperative that every ten minutes you go back, and sit there for few more minutes.

- Keep on doing this for two days. Is it time consuming? Not really, if you want to see your pets again.
- And before you know it, they will come back, and they will rub against you, and you are going to feel it, and you will never ever forget that feeling.
- This would be their farewell to you...

*** *** ***

51. Levels of the Mind
"Iama"
⌘ ⌘ ⌘

I. Definition and introduction
II. "All humans have more than one brain"

I. Definition and introduction:
A term referring to the concept of the different "Levels of the Mind".
According to many authors and thinkers, the human brain is a depot of all knowledge we have acquired so far.
This is not totally correct, according to the Book of Ramadosh. Ulema Oppenheimer said verbatim, as is and unedited: "The physical brain, or in other words, the brain of a human being living here on Earth is one of the multiple layers of an infinite series of knowledge and experience acquired by a person in and outside the barrier of time and space.
Meaning that every single human being, regardless of the level of his or her intelligence and social status has an infinite number of other brains "Minds" fully operational in different and multiple spheres, times and spaces.
And this includes the landscape of our Solar System, and other universes' systems. This is the cause and effect of the creation of the Universe and Man.

II. "All humans have more than one brain":
Man cannot be separated from the universe, because he is a vital and primordial part of its molecules. In other words, a person can be very intelligent and extremely important in this life, and in the same time, he can be a total ignorant and unimportant in other life that co-exists simultaneously somewhere else in the universe." He added "here on Earth you might be an amateur

musician, and in other world you are a conductor of symphonic orchestra, or even equal to Mozart.

In each dimension, and this includes stars and planets, you as a human being you live a separate life, and you have a totally independent brain.

Some Masters are fully capable of synchronizing both, and even more..."

*** *** ***

52. Interpretation of Messages Sent to the Conduit "Haridu", "Haridu-ilmu"
⌘ ⌘ ⌘

I. Definition
II. Ulema Rabbi Mordechai explains Haridu-Conduit Equation

I. Definition:
Interpretation of messages sent to the "Conduit" in an Anunnaki's or a human's brain cell. Also, it applies to missing or misinterpreting a message by the Conduit.

II. Mordechai explains Haridu–Conduit Equation:
Ulema Mordechai said verbatim:
- "First of all, you have to remember that your mind (Your brain) has nothing to do with your Conduit. Even though, your brain is functioning wonderfully and you are doing great things in your life, not all the cells in your brain have been used.
- There are so many regions in our brain that have not been explored yet by science.
- In those many unexplored regions of the brain, are so many cells yet to be discovered, located and localized. And above all, we need to learn how they function.
- In that mysterious undiscovered region of the brain, the Conduit exists. It could be in the right or left side of your brain, or just adjacent to line dividing the two parts.
- In the Conduit, there are so many cells, each one with a very defined and particular extraordinary faculty/power, that needs to be activated.
- For instance, one cell triggers the faculty of reading others' thoughts, another cell (Or cells) is responsible for the faculty of teleportation, so on.

- If those cells are not activated, you will not be able to do all those wonderful things.
- So, you have to consider the Conduit as a bank where so many cells are deposited.
- And there are hundreds of thousands of cells deposited in the Conduit.
- Each cell has a precise function and an invisible location.
- This means that the Conduit can do so many things, if cells are activated. It would be impossible in one lifespan to develop and activate all the cells.
- Three or four fully activated cells is more than enough. With four activated cells you can do four great miracles by earth's standards.
- But for the cell to produce this extraordinary power, the cell must be able first to understand what you want to do.
- For instance, you cannot tell or command your cell "go ahead and make me fly or let me learn a new language in one hour."
- You should first learn how to send your command to your cell. There is a technique for this.
- Your Ulema teacher knows how to put you on the right track.
- Let's assume you have sent a message (A thought, a wish) to your cell. What's next? Well, the message enters your Conduit. Your conduit acting as a supervisor, and as the main receiver reads your message and directs your message to the appropriate cell.
- Your Conduit knows which cell is activated and designed to comply with your request.
- Instantly, the cell receives the Conduit transfer (Meaning your message.)
- Then what? The cell reads your message.
- If your message was sent correctly, then the cell will accept it and give it a code. So, if in the future you ask again your Conduit to do the same thing you have asked in the past, the cell will execute your request in a fraction of a second.
- In other words, each request is coded, and stored in your cell.

- Only coded messages are stored in your Conduit.
- How would you know if you have or have not sent a message correctly to your Conduit? You will know right away. It is very simple. If you have not been trained, you wouldn't know where and how to start in the first place.
- This is the reason why your Conduit did not catch your message(s).
- You asked "Does this mean that my Conduit is not receiving clear messages from me? And the answer is yes! Your Conduit received something, a thought, a feeling, a wish, a request, call it whatever you want, but your message was not clear to your Conduit, because you did not send your message according to the rules.
- What are these rules?
- They are explained below. But continue to read this first.
- And then you asked: "And how can I send clear messages my Conduit can catch and understand?
- You have to use the "Transmission of Mind" technique. Practice this technique before you send messages to your Conduit. For example, in the past, the SOS (Morse Code) was used by ships, planes, military troops and others. The person who has sent the message (Morse) knew the Code; he/she knew how to tap it.
- Each word had a code...one dot, two dots, three dots, one dash, two dashes, three dashes, one dit, two dits, one space, two spaces, three spaces, etc.
- There is a sequence of pulses and marks. And the person who received the message knew how what these dots, and dashes meant.
- This is how and why he/she was able to read the message or decipher it, if it was a secret message.
- Your Conduit works exactly in the same way.
- Your Ulema teacher will tell you exactly what dots and sequences to use.
- If your Conduit is hundred percent awake, meaning open (After training completion), the Conduit will immediately interpret and translate and understand your dots, dashes and sequences.
- Consider those dashes and dots a "Password", a logging-in information, a key to open the contact with your

Conduit, just like the password you use to open your computer or have access to some websites.
- In the Book of Ramadosh, you will find several passages referring to the brain waves and mind frequencies, and some techniques used to direct thoughts and mind energies.
- Your Conduit has its own mode. As long as your Conduit is not activated, it remains free of your control. Once your Conduit is activated, you become the stimulus and the manager of your Conduit.
- The Conduit works partially when it is not activated.
- And partially means reacting by not acting.
- The Conduit functions all the time regardless of your state of awareness, enlightenment or readiness. But it will not give you data and information.
- Everything the Conduit finds or retrieves is always instantly deposited/stored in its compound.
- You will not find what's in there, until the Conduit is fully activated.
- Consider it for now as a depot of knowledge; a sort of a personal bank account where your daily balance is constantly increasing, however, you are not allowed to have access to your bank account.
- So, nothing is lost.
- Your Conduit collects and stores information all the time, and from various sources, times, and spheres.

*** *** ***

53. Plasmic Halo Surrounding the Physical Body "Hatani"
⌘⌘⌘

I. Definition
II. The concept
III. The Hatani "Protection Shield"
IV. Hatani and Khuch "Kush-Ra": Protection against physical threats and harms

53. Plasmic Halo Surrounding the Physical Body "Hatani"
⌘⌘⌘

I. Definition
II. The concept
III. The Hatani "Protection Shield"
IV. Hatani and Khuch "Kush-Ra": Protection against physical threats and harms

*** *** ***

I. Definition:
Usually referred to a plasmic halo surrounding the physical body of an Anunnaki-Ulema. From Hatani, derived the Akkadian verb Hatanu, which means to shelter. Hatani is closely related to the Anunnaki-Ulema Baridu technique.
Baridu is the Anunnaki-Ulema term for the act of zooming into an astral body or a Double.

II. The concept:

- The initiated and enlightened ones can zoom into their other bodies, and acquire Anunnaki supernatural faculties.
- I have used the words supernatural faculties instead of supernatural powers, because the enlightened and initiated ones are peaceful, and do not use aggressive physical power, or brutal force to achieve their goals.
- The use of violence against humans and animals, even aggressive thoughts and harmful intentions annihilate all chances to acquire Anunnaki's extraordinary faculties.
- Your Double can easily read your thoughts.

- If your thoughts are malicious, your Double will prevent you from zooming yourself into its ethereal molecules.
- Therefore, you have to control your temper, remain calm, and show serenity in your thoughts, intentions and actions.
- You Double is delicate, even though it can accomplish the toughest missions and penetrate the thickest barriers.
- Any indication of violence or ill intention triggers a pulse that blocks your passage to the ethereal sphere of your Double.
- Once you enter your Double, you will be able to use it in so many beautiful and effective ways as:
  1- A protective shield against danger,
  2- An effective apparatus to protect yourself in hostile and dangerous situations,
  3- A tool to develop your abilities to learn many languages, and enhance your artistic creativity,
  4- A stimulus to increase the capacity of your memory,
  5- Instrument to heal wounds and internal injuries. No, you will not become a surgeon, but you will be able to stop internal bleeding, and eliminate pain,
  6- A vehicle to visit distant places and even enter restricted areas for good causes. The possibilities are endless.

Once you are in a perfect harmony with your Double, and your physical organism is elevated to a higher vibrational level through your union with your Double, you will be able to walk through solid substances such as walls, sheets of glasses and metal.

You become effective in controlling metal and de-fragmenting molecules of any substance. This will allow you to transmute, change and alter the properties of any object known to mankind. But if you use these supernatural faculties to hurt others, or for personal and selfish gain, you will loose them for good, and you will be accountable for such malicious use in the other dimension. And this could delay your entrance through the Ba'ab.

III. The Hatani "Protection Shield":

Excerpts from Ulema Kira'at; Ulema Govinda said about the protection against threats and dangers (Verbatim):
- Only those who have learned and developed esoteric Ulema techniques can use their Double as a shield.
- However, a novice or a sincere student who is searching for the ultimate paranormal truth, and who has revealed a high standard of spirituality and goodness will be able to use the Double, once he/she has completed the Ulema studies.
- At a novice stage, the Double is alive and well, and is fully aware of your existence, but as a novice, you are not aware of its existence, because you have not established a rapport with your Double.
- Once, a rapport has been established with your Double, your Conduit will throw an invisible protective shield around you.
- But was is a shield? Is it a physical barrage? A protective tool or a device similar to the fibreglass or a metal shield police use in riots?
- The answer is no.
- The shield functions in so many different ways your brain cannot comprehend. However, I will try to explain to you one of the protective measures a shield uses in threatening situations.
- The Ulema after years of study and practice, and following the instructions of the Book of Rama-Dosh, became capable of creating a sphere (Or zone) around them that resembles a halo.
- Some call this halo a "Bubble".
- The halo surrounds their physical body.
- In the halo, exist molecules and particles charged with high atomic and sub-atomic density (No, not nuclear devices!), i.e. energy.
- This energy is denser in its composition than any of the molecules and particles that physically create and constitute any physical action or movement against an Ulema's body.
- Ulema's energy changes constantly and transmutes itself into higher or lower molecules and particles density, according to their surroundings and needs.

- Because of the Ulema's denser atomic substance, nothing can penetrate the halo surrounding them.
- You have to remember, that everything in the universe is composed from molecules and particles.
- For instance, if you throw a punch at an Ulema, you put in your punch a certain amount of energy and physical effort. The energy and the physical effort are composed from molecules.
- These molecules are denser in their composition than the molecules floating around the Ulema, and thus cannot penetrate their halo and reach their bodies.
- This is why people can't go through walls. Our bodies molecules need "to shrink" and "transmute" themselves into thinner vibrations, to allow us to go through walls.
- The non-physical entity (Double) you have mentioned is not totally non-physical.
- It changes. It materializes and dematerializes.
- The Double can project itself as a physical entity. And it takes on multiple appearances ranging from holographic to multi-dimensional presences.
- However, the materialistic apparition does not last very long in a three-dimensional sphere, because its bio-etco-plasma energy is consumed rapidly.
- **a**-Your Double is extremely intelligent and alert, and it senses things around you. Things currently happening and those en route.
- **b**-Your Double knows right away if what is coming at you is safe or dangerous.
- **c**-If the Double detects a threatening situation, it sends an alert to your Conduit.
- **d**-Your Conduit receives the message from your Double. (Note: Sometimes, it is simultaneously, and/or your Open Conduit understands the situation on its own, without the help of your Double.)
- **e**-Your Conduit acts on its own and guides you instantly to a safer position. Call it whatever you want, instinct, an inner feeling, etc...it does not matter what you call it.
- **f**-At the same time, your Conduit emits vibes aimed at the source of the threat to bock it.

- **g**-At this very moment, your Open Conduit and your Double act in unison.
- **h**-In a fraction of a second, the attacker or the negative vibes aimed at you is diverted. Nothing can penetrate the halo around you. If you practice and master the Baridu technique, you will be able to block any threat."

*** *** ***

IV. Protection against physical threats and harms "Hatani and Khuch, Kush-Ra"

Note: The following is taken from a Q&A during a Master's Kira'at. Part of the text overlaps with a text mentioned above. This was intentional, because we do not recall precisely when and how the Q&A and the Master's Kira'at occurred in the remote past. We tried to reconstruct the events to the best of our ability, so please excuse us for this unavoidable repetition.

Khuch "Kush-Ra" is a term for the energy that animates the "Double" of a human being. From Khuch, derived the Kabalistic and Hebrew term Khuch-ha-guf "Kuch-ha-guf", which means the astral body of a man. According to the Ulema, the Double's energy serves also as a protection shield against all sorts of threats and dangers.

During an Ulema Kira'at, a student asked the Ulema: "Regarding the Baridu technique... you said that "Once you enter your Double, you will be able to use it in so many beautiful and effective ways as a protective shield against danger, and an effective apparatus to protect yourself in hostile and dangerous situations.

My questions is:

How a non-physical entity that does not live on Earth can protect me from physical threats?

If this is true, then the President of the United States and the Secretary of State should get rid of their bodyguards and hire a Double? It does not make sense!"

The Ulema replied verbatim:
"Protection against threats and dangers: First of all, you have to remember that people of power, politicians, *et al*, are neither spiritual people, nor adepts of metaphysical studies.
They spend more time campaigning, shaking hands, and giving speeches than developing spiritual and paranormal abilities.
So bodyguards remain a necessity. They should stay around.

Only those who have learned and developed esoteric Ulema techniques can use their Double as a shield. However, a novice or a sincere student who is searching for the ultimate paranormal truth, and who has revealed a high standard of spirituality and goodness will be able to use the Double, once he/she has completed the Ulema studies.
At your stage, your Double is alive and well, and is fully aware of your existence, but YOU are not aware of its existence, because either you do not believe in a Double, or you have not established a rapport with your Double.
Once, a rapport has been established with your Double, your Conduit will throw an invisible protective shield around you. But was is a shield?
Is it a physical barrage?
A protective tool or a device similar to the fibreglass or a metal shield police use in riots?
The answer is no. The shield functions in so many different ways your brain cannot comprehend. However, I will try to explain to you one of the protective measures a shield uses in threatening situations.

The Ulema after years of study and practice, and following the instructions of the Book of Rama-Dosh, became capable of creating a sphere (Or zone) around them that resembles a halo. Some call this halo a "Bubble".
The halo surrounds their physical body.
In the halo, exist molecules and particles charged with high atomic and sub-atomic density (No, not nuclear devices!), i.e. energy. This energy is denser in its composition than any of the molecules and particles that physically create and constitute any physical action or movement against an Ulema's body.
Ulema's energy changes constantly and transmutes itself into higher or lower molecules/particles density, according to their surroundings and needs.

Because of the Ulema's denser atomic substance, nothing can penetrate the halo surrounding them. You have to remember, that everything in the universe is composed from molecules and particles.

For instance, if you throw a punch at an Ulema, you put in your punch a certain amount of energy and physical effort. The energy and the physical effort are composed from molecules. These molecules are denser in their composition than the molecules floating around the Ulema, and thus cannot penetrate their halo and reach their bodies.

*** *** ***

54. Shape-shifting "Ibra-Anu"
⌘⌘⌘

I. Definition and introduction
II. Anunnaki's shape-shifting

I. Definition and introduction:
For extraterrestrials, shape-shifting is necessary.
Ambar Anati said verbatim (As is a nd unedited): "Shape-shifting includes skin color change, organs size, general physical appearances, but not the functionality of the body.
The Anunnaki can easily shape-shift themselves.
This is necessary for climatic and atmospheric reasons.
Each planet has its own climate, temperature and atmosphere. Consequently the body must adapt to these environment conditions.

II. Anunnaki's shape-shifting:
When they visit Earth, the Anunnaki slightly change their physical appearances, not so much, because in general, they look like us, except their eyes are much bigger, and their height is far more superior and taller to the size and height of humans. Some Anunnaki are 9 foot tall. Even their women are extremely tall by human standard.
Some women are 8 foot tall. When they travel to other planets, minor changes are required.
For instance, when they get out of their galaxy and visit the planets Niftar, Marshan-Haloum and Ibra-Anu, they change the color of their skin, and the shape of their hands.

On Niftar (Niftari), inhabitants have grey-blue color skin and 3 fingers in each hand. The fingers are long, thin and beneath the skin, there are millions of microscopic hair filaments and pores (orifices) that help them hold on slippery surfaces like glass and wet areas. Anunnaki look very different from the Zetas and the numerous alien races that have visited the earth. In this context, they never appear or manifest like reptilians or short "Greys". It is easy to recognize an Anunnaki, because he usually appears like a tall warrior; his vest is made out of thin layers of metal called "Handar".

He wears a long robe "Arbiya" of dark colors and underneath, it a sort of pans with wide contour. On his wrist, you always notice a navigation tool. Many of the extraterrestrial races wear tight outfits, almost glued to their skin. Anunnaki don't. The "Greys" are notorious for shape-shifting. They can appear like a reptile, an insect and even like humans. The Anunnaki can transmute and manipulate their bodies if needed.

This happens very rarely. And in many instances, they don't need to do so, because they are already known by so many galactic and outer-galactic civilizations, and seen by inhabitants of millions and millions of stars, planets and moons. They are superstars in their own rights.

Aliens of lower dimensions need to manipulate their bodiy-type to enter the atmosphere of other planets, particularly underwater and a multitude of underground environments and habitats.

This is exactly what happens all the time with the "Greys" who live on earth and work with scientists in restricted areas such as underground genetic labs, and military research centers and bases. One of their striking characteristics is claustrophobia.

*** *** ***

Bringing Youth to Your Face
"Hatori-shabah"
⌘ ⌘ ⌘

I. Definition
II. Ulema Suleiman Al Bak'r explains the concept

I. Definition:
It refers to various phases of youth brought to a person via the practice of the Anunnaki-Ulema Daemat-Afnah technique.
It is closely related to Daemat-Afnah, which is a term for longevity, and halting the process of aging.

It is composed of two words:
a-Daemat, which means longevity.
b-Afnah, which means many things, including health, fecundity, and longevity.
According to the Anunnaki-Ulema, we are not programmed to age.
By practicing the Daemat-Afnah, a person will regain his/her youth, and his/her face will look 37 year old.

II. Ulema Suleiman Al Bak'r explains the concept:
On the subject, Ulema Suleiman Al Bak'r said (Verbatim):

- "You have to practice the technique for at least one full year. You will not see any improvement or any result before 12 months. I will explain to you what is going to happen step by step.
- For the first 6 months. You will not notice any change on your face.
- At the end of the seventh month, you will begin to feel that some of your facial muscles are getting stronger. A

strange and a new sensation you have never felt before in your whole life.
- Your face will look cleaner and firmer.
- Some of the wrinkles under your eyes will disappear. In rare instances, they would not.
- Not all the wrinkles will disappear if you stop practicing.
- At the end of 12 months, you will notice that you eyes have gained vitality. They will look sharper.
- Your eyes will glitter with a sign of good health.
- At the end of 12 months, you will notice that your face's skin is healthier, and almost 90% of your wrinkles (large and small) have diminished.
- The dermatologic results have no side effect.
- A certain incomprehensible inner strength will energize your whole body.
- After 13 months of practice, the face you had when you were 37 starts to reappear gradually. You will not believe what you are seeing.
- This change is usually accompanied by sizeable increase in physical dynamism and mental vitality.
- Your face is younger, almost 100%.
- Only your face gets younger, not your neck, body or any other part of your body.
- Your grey hair will stay grey.
- If you are bold, you will stay bold."
- You will keep your new face for a very very long time, as long as you keep a good diet, and you eat well.

*** *** ***

56. The Ability of Observing Entities Fluctuation
"Idartari"
⌘⌘⌘

I. Definition
II. Pets and children ability to see non-physical entities

I. Definition:
A term for the act of observing "Entities Fluctuation".
Anunnaki Ulema Al Baker explained (As is and unedited): "Fluctuation is a signal that something or some living form is around you, but with your limited physical senses and faculties, you are unable to see it in its real appearance.

II. Pets and children ability to see non-physical entities:
Pets like cats and dogs can see non-physical entities.
But this is not limited only to animals. Children when they are little can also sense and see these entities, and in fact, they do enjoy watching these entities and conversing with them. Parents should not discourage or punish their children when they tell them stories about ghosts and "unseen friends".

We can learn a lot from pets and children, just by watching how they react in the presence of these entities, and by taking notes.
At the beginning, this would not make any sense to many of us, but we take notes, if we are patient, and we start to compare these notes following several events, our mind will open up, and a part of our "Conduit" will be activated. These entities are not the product of the imagination of a child.
They do exist in multiple etheric and even plasmic form.

But our eyes, more precisely our brain is unable to perceive them. Unfortunately, children lose this wonderful faculty as they grow up. Animals don't."
And he added, "It is so beneficial to have pets at home. The time will come and you will realize that a presence of a pet in your home is in fact a blessing."

*** *** ***

57. Extraterrestrials in the Book of Ramadosh
"Ezakarfalki",
"E-zakar-falki"
⌘⌘⌘

I. Definition and introduction
II. Evolution of the extraterrestrials and the human races
III. Extraterrestrial races populated the Earth
IV. Extraterrestrials of the sea (Underwater)
V. Senses of the extraterrestrials
VI. Talking to extraterrestrials

57. Extraterrestrials in the Book of Ramadosh "Ezakarfalki", "E-zakar-falki"

I. Definition and introduction
II. Evolution of the extraterrestrials and the human races
III. Extraterrestrial races populated the Earth
IV. Extraterrestrials of the sea (Underwater)
V. Senses of the extraterrestrials
VI. Talking to extraterrestrials

I. Definition and introduction:
Term for extraterrestrials as mentioned in the Book of Rama-Dosh.
Per contra, inhabitants of planet Earth are called Ezakarerdi or Ezakar.Ki.
In terrestrial vocabulary, extraterrestrial(s) is a term applied to any entity(ies), object(s), substance(s), life-form(s), intelligence, and presence that have originated from beyond planet Earth. Grosso modo, referred to as alien(s).
Contemporary ufology etymology added extraterrestrial origins coming from outer-space, other planets, stars, galaxies, and dimensions.

The word extraterrestrial is composed from three words:
- **a**-Extra, which is derived from the Latin word Extra, which means outside; additional; beyond.
- **b**-Terrestri, derived from the Latin Terrestris, which means pertaining to earth; belonging to earth; earthly; made out of earth, itself derived from the Latin words Terranum and Terrenum, which are derived from the word Terra, which means earth; ground; piece of land; soil.

(Note: From the Latin word Terrenum, derived the French word Terrain; and from the French word derived the English word terrain.)

c-Al, an English addition.
Note: The Latin word Terra originally derived from the Arabic word "Tourab" (Terrab), which means dirt; dust; earth, itself derived from the Arabic word Tourba (Terrba), which means a piece of land, originally derived from the Ana'kh word Turbah, pronounced Toorbaah, which means dirt from planet Earth.

In the Sumerian/Akkadian epics and mythologies, the words dirt and earth refer to clay; the very clay found in abundance in ancient Iraq that was used by the Anunnaki to genetically create the human race.

II. Evolution of the extraterrestrials and the human races:
Ulema Maximillien de Lafayette said, the evolution of aliens, and the extraterrestrial races on many galaxies evolved inter-dimensionally by copying, duplicating, and cloning themselves and fertilizing their own genes.
On other planets, more advanced extraterrestrial civilizations multiply and prosper through the development of brain's waves and thoughts frequencies.
They did not need to immigrate to other planets in order to survive, and/or to recreate (Reshape) themselves, as mistakenly claimed by some ufologists, extraterrestrialogists, mediums, and channelers, for they did not encounter insurmountable ecological or bio-organic catastrophes on their own planets or stars.

Zetas and Anunnaki did alter their genetics but, not for survival purposes or for intra-planetary travel-immigration readiness reasons. The alteration came as cause and effect, much needed to reach a higher level of awareness and scientific advancement.

III. Extraterrestrial races populated the Earth:
Some 300,000 years before the creation of the cities of "The Women of Lights," forty-six different races of humans and quasi-humans populated the earth.
The greatest numbers were found in Africa, Madagascar, Indonesia, Brazil, and Australia. These quasi-human races died

out not because of famine, ecological catastrophes, or acts of war, but because of the disintegration of the very molecules and composition of their cells.

The Anunnaki created the 'final form' of human beings, and all of us are their descendants.

IV. Extraterrestrials of the sea (Underwater):

According to Sinhar Ambar Anati, the extraterrestrials of the sea are not our ancestors and creators, the Anunnaki. They belong to a different race; one of the 46 different alien races that have visited the earth at its dawn. Only 7 specific races remained on Earth. They have many things in common, and share non-physical similarities, but are different from the Anunnaki.

According to ufology literature, the aliens who currently work with terrestrial scientists have extraterrestrial physiognomy, totally alien to the human race. The original Anunnaki no longer live on earth.

They left our planet thousands of years ago. However, many of their off springs, bloodlines, descendants and hybrid remnants live among us, today.

Ulema Sadqi said: "The Anunnaki are not very much different from the human beings. They are not reptilians at all, and they don't look like the Zeta Reticulians, as erroneously depicted in the West. They have a human shape, yet they are capable to shape shifting when needed."

V. Senses of the extraterrestrials:

Anunnaki-Ulema Wah Lin stated that the extraterrestrials have an astonishing range of senses; for instance:
- **a**-The Artyrians have 13 different kinds of senses, ranging from physio-biological to mental-sensorial, yet, they are neither psychosomatic nor neurological.
- **b**-The Naryans have 17 senses.
- **c**-The Anunnaki have 26 extra-senses and a multitude of meta-bio-organic faculties."

Ulema Li adds: "Some of the most fascinating senses are:
- **a**-The ability of freeing themselves from the limitation of time and space and sensing the "ultra dimension"; in other words, they are able to feel and sense the infinitesimal frequencies that constitute the dividing

waves or walls between each dimension and/or multiple universes. Those dividing lines are waves and they expand and react spatially like rubber bands. There are no other words or expressions in the human vocabularies we can use to describe these "existences".

- **b**-They can totally eliminate the effect of heat and cold and mentally regulate the temperature degrees of the environment in any sphere. Also they can adjust others bodies' temperature for health and therapeutic reasons because they can sense the body's weaknesses and strengths.

In terrestrial terms, they can see the aura. But it goes beyond aura, because aura is produced bio-organically and can be detected either visually or through scientific apparatus.

VI. Talking to extraterrestrials:

Anunnaki and extraterrestrials have no intention whatsoever in engaging into a dialogue with ordinary human beings. If they have an agenda, and/or are on a mission, they either abduct (Not the Anunnaki) humans, or directly contact scientists working with them in secret facilities, laboratories and bases.

Anunnaki do not talk tête-à-tête with humans, nor convey their messages on a personal basis. And most certainly, Anunnaki do not abduct humans. However, direct and personal contact did happen with aliens. They were the "Greys".
But this occurrence is extremely rare. Ulema Al Bakri said: " And when and if it happens, extraterrestrials would not pronounce one word and walk away, or stutter as some contactees reported", including one famous contactee in Switzerland who made headlines worldwide and became the messenger of the Lyrans on earth. When aliens contact (So to speak) or encounter a human being, they usually complete sentences and engage into a dialogue, even though, the dialogue is short, and their words are incomprehensible, and the voice is mechanic and fuzzy.

In some instances, the aliens transmit their messages mentally, not telepathically, because for the telepathic phenomenon to occur, you need two telepathic people, and most certainly contactees who are regular folks are neither gifted nor trained telepaths. You cannot talk to another person on your cellular phone, if the other party does not have one.

Do you want to try? Same thing applies to telepathy; it needs two telepathic stations, fully operational and fully capable of sending and receiving messages.

The human brain did not yet reach this level. Although some preliminary forms of telepathy between humans were noticed in rare instances. Extraterrestrials are capable of speaking and understanding many languages, including our own.

They assimilate and "compute" words, sentences and physical expressions with mathematical formulas and numerical values.

Some extraterrestrials have limited vocal chords capabilities, but they can very quickly acquire additional vocal faculties, and earth dialects by rewinding sounds and vibes. Contrary to what many contactees and others claim or depict, extraterrestrials from higher dimensions do not talk like computerized machines.

They have their own language but also they can absorb and assimilate all the languages on earth in a blink of an eye via the reception and emission of a spatial memory.

*** *** ***

58. The First stage of the Afterlife "Hattari"
⌘ ⌘ ⌘

I. Definition
II. Description

I. Definition:
The first stage of the afterlife during the 40 day period following death. In that stage, a new life-form develops in the mind of deceased people.

II. Description:
Note from A. Doudnikova:
A brief description of Hattari was given by a lady (Who apparently was an Ulema) to her beloved son. Here is an excerpt from the "Forbidden Book of Ramadosh", based on the original work of Maximillien de Lafayette:
The scene is between Germain Lumiere, an Ulema from France who has just lost his mother. It appeared later on, that his mother was an Ulema too, but she has never told him that, for reasons we don't know.
Two days after she passed away in Paris, his mother appeared to him during her funeral, as she has promised him.
The young Ulema asked his mother lots of question about the after-life, and what is she doing there. Herewith, a brief excerpt from their conversation:

Location: Cemetery of Père-Lachaise, Paris, France.
Time: In the afternoon, during the funeral of Countess....mother of Germain.
Personages:
1-The deceased mother appears as a spirit and talks to her son Germain, while her physical body is in the coffin.
2-Germain in tears talking to his dead mother for the last time.

3-Sylvie: She is Germain's sister.

Excerpt below: Germain is telling us what they talked about at the funeral.

"I returned to Mama, who was looking sadly at Sylvie. It's really too bad I can't talk to her," Mama said to me, "but some day, of course, she will know, like everyone else. Ah, well, let's go to the more secluded areas. We don't want people to think you are talking to yourself."

We wandered around the cemetery. Père Lachaise, is one of the most beautiful cemeteries in the world, full of trees, impressive statues, and old tombstones. Shady lanes provided privacy, and we could talk freely.

"So tell me about your experience in the Afterlife, Mama," I said.

"I have not been there very long, you know, but time and space play a different role there, and also, my training allows me to know what it is really like and what will happen next," said Mama. "You will also know, when the time comes."

"Doesn't everyone know?"

"No, many of the dead don't realize that they are dead. They don't seem to see the border between life and afterlife. These people can be very anxious.

They sometimes try to get back to Earth, meet their loved ones, and they are very upset when the living cannot see them."

"So what happens to them?"

"The guides, spirits of higher dimensions, help them realize that they are dead. Sometimes, if persons have a real need to go back to Earth to accomplish something, the guides are saddened by their pain, and allow them to go back, manifest, and complete their task. Once they do that, they can come back, much happier and calmer. It only happens once, of course, but after that they are ready to adjust to the afterlife."

"What is it like, over there? Were you scared when you passed on?"

"There is nothing frightening about the afterlife," said Mama. "It is very much like earth, but peaceful, much more beautiful, and there is no strife or violence of any kind. To the departed, who have shed their bodies and are occupying a new body, it is as physical as the earth is to the living.

Everyone is healthy, there is no disease, no pain, no violence. There are cities with streets and buildings, gardens and parks, countryside – all seems normal, like a poetic interpretation of life. What you see here is visual projections.

You see millions of real people, coming and going in huge waves. There is much to do, since the place you come to first is no more than a quick stop. You only stay here for twenty to thirty days, some times forty days, and then move on."

"Do they know where they are going?"

"It depends. Most people cannot see what is ahead of them, only what is behind them. But they always move on to a higher phase."

"So naturally they are a bit scared of the unknown."

"Yes, some of them experience anxiety. That is what the twenty to thirty days period is for, deciding what needs and things to be done. And they are helped by the guides, or by people who chose to stay longer in this place."

"So you can stay there longer?"

"Yes, there are various options, of course. One option is to go to the place you have created when you built your "Minzar" and planned a place of rest and happiness.
Many people choose to go there for a while – it is up to them how long they would stay there. Time is not really a very important issue where we are. It seems to me that time has stopped. You can stay there forever if you like it very much."

"The place created with the Minzar must be very appealing to most people, I should say," I said. "It's custom made for your own happiness."

"Yes, and the person already has friends, a place to stay, things to do, anything he or she likes best. It's a good option. But eventually, I would say one should try to evolve into the higher dimensions. You don't know what you miss unless you see it."

"When I built the Minzar, Rabbi Mordechai told me that I could not stay in the place I created for too long, since the energy would dissipate and the living body will call me back. But I suppose it's different when one is dead."

"Yes, since this is now part of the depot of knowledge located in your brain, which was created by the Minzar experience. It is your Spatial Memory, my son."

"So you plan to move on after the thirty days?"

"Yes. It is as it should be, and I want to evolve into the higher dimensions. But as I promised, I will come back for you and be your guide when it is your time to follow me. Think about it as a short, though necessary separation, but temporary all the same. What it all comes down to, Germain, is that there is no death. And the afterlife offers so many opportunities for new growth, new knowledge. There is nothing to fear."

"Will you see Papa? Will I see him when I go there?"

"Of course we will. Do not worry and do not mourn me, Germain."

"I will try not to, Mama. I promise."

"Well, my son, I will be leaving now. No need to say goodbye. Rather, au revoir."

I closed my eyes, not wishing to see her leave, and felt something brush my cheek as if she kissed me. When I opened my eyes, there was no sign of her. She was gone. I went home and helped Sylvie attend to the visitors; I have never felt so numb."

*** *** ***

59. The Fourth Dimension "Chabkaradi"
⌘ ⌘ ⌘

I. Definition
II. Explanation

I. Definition:
Name of the Fourth sphere on the cosmic net.
Herewith an excerpt of the definition, meaning and dimensions of Chabkaradi, from Ulema Maximillien de Lafayette's Kira'at: Translated verbatim from the Ulemite and Ana'kh languages, word for word (Unedited).

II. Explanation:
- 1-The 4th dimension is where the mind navigates freely.
- 2-Your physical body cannot enter the 4th dimension.
- 3-However, the righteous Ulema can physically enter the 4th dimension for a very short time.
- 4-Short time means less than 40 days.
- 5-Any living Ulema who stays for more than 40 days in the 4th dimension will disintegrate, and will never be able to return to earth again.
- 6-In the 4th dimension, there is a real reflection of everything that exists on earth.
- 7-A real reflection means an identical presence in substance and properties of all physical things on earth. But they exist at a different vibrational level.
- 8-A vibrational level is what constitutes the substance of any object or matter in the universe, including thoughts, intentions, and events that did not happen yet.
- 9-The vibrations on earth can be detected, but not all of them.

- **10-**The mind vibrations and waves frequencies can be detected on earth. But the vibrations that have created the mind in the first place are undetectable by humans.
- **11-**If for some unknown reasons, you were able to enter the 4th dimension, and if you were not guided by a higher presence such as supreme entities, highly advanced non–terrestrial beings, etc., your body will be exposed to tremendous physical and non-physical pressures.
    This could cause loss of memory and blindness. It did happen, and we are mentioning it here for additional learning, but it is not useful to elaborate further on this situation.
- **12-**Now, if you were brought to the 4th dimension by non-terrestrial benevolent beings, your journey will be very pleasant and enlightening. This could happen in two ways, and only two ways:
- **a-**Via a galactic multi-dimensional Markabah. This spaceship does not travel or traverse distances and dimensions. It "jumps" from one time pocket to another time pocket on the map of the universe. In front of the spaceship, time and space as two separate dimensions cease to exist. They cancel each other.
    This allows the spaceship to reach higher spheres at an incredible speed way beyond the comprehension of human beings. Behind the spaceship, time and space open and close up as soon as the spaceship exits from the time-space tunnel that allowed the spaceship to reach the 4th dimension, or the parallel one.
- **b-**Via Tay Al Ard technique or the projection of mind. Only Ulema and the enlightened ones who learned these techniques from non-terrestrial beings can do that.
- **13-**The 4th dimension is incomprehensible, because it has a semi start-line, but not a finish-line.
- **14-**Beyond the 4th dimension exists the 5th dimension which is the realm of the purified entities. No physical substances exist in the 5th dimension, only their codes.
- **15-**Yet, in the 4th dimension, many physical forms retain their physical properties.
- **16-**Humans will spend many many years in the 4th dimension before they reach a higher one.

- **17**-Many humans (Minds or Souls) could get lost around the perimeter of the 4th dimension.
- **18**-Humans who just arrive in spirit or in mind to the 4th dimension have two choices and decisions to make within 40 days:
- **a**-To stay in the 4th dimension and evolve or
- **b**-To return to earth.
- **19**-Those who decide to stay in the 4th dimension will be taken to an area similar to the Anunnaki's Miraya Hall.
- **20**-They will receive orientation and guidance from supreme beings who come to visit and lecture from much higher dimensions.
- **21**-Those who began to progress and evolve spiritually in the 4th dimension will be acknowledged. Their spiritual progress will elevate their mental vibrations, thus allowing them to see loved ones, and to enjoy the company of delightful higher beings.
- **22**-It could take a person thousands of years (in terrestrial term) to evolve. But time does not exist in higher dimensions, not even the perception of time.
- **23**-Some evolve rapidly and elevate themselves to the 5th dimension, the sphere of absolute beauty and happiness.
- **24**-Almost all human beings reach the 5th dimension, except those who caused so much damage, pains and sufferings to others. No, they will not burn in fire. There is no hell in the world beyond, but the mental-spiritual pain is as atrocious as the physical pain...

*** *** ***

60. State of the Human Mind After Death
"Zrah-Amru"
⌘ ⌘ ⌘

I. Definition
II. The Ulema explain

I. Definition:
A term referring to the status of the mind in the afterlife vis-à-vis one's previous commitment on Earth. This situation is explained in a Q&A of one of the Ulema's Kira'ats (Readings and lectures).

II. The Ulema explain:
A student asked the Ulema:
Question: If Bashar (Humans) can reach immortality and live for ever in the other world where they reunite with their loved ones, what would be the position, reaction and obligations of a widow who married other men after the death of her first husband, when she meets them afterlife in other dimension?
The honorable Ulema's answer:
- Since we do believe that life continues after death, multiple marriages could cause a state of mental confusion, and perhaps embarrassment for the deceased widow who remarried after the death of the departed spouse...this could happen upon meeting multiple husbands or wives in the early stage in the Fourth dimension.
- But once the Mind is purified, and as we progress mentally and spiritually, we begin to see and understand the situation very differently...
- In higher dimensions, such as the afterlife, the Mind functions, sees and understands things very very differently from the way we were accustomed to on earth.
- The deceased continues to live after death as a Mind.

- The Mind retains terrestrial memory, even though the Mind has lost all sensorial properties.
- The Mind cannot alter the past. We are stuck with the memory of everything we have done on earth. Only the Anunnaki who created us genetically can alter the past of the person they have created. And by altering the past, the Anunnaki can erase all kinds of memories, including related events that occurred in one particular dimension.
- This is applicable only when a person has been created on earth by an Anna.Ki (Anunnaki). I said on earth, because there are so many different beings who were created by other creators governing other planets, stars and dimensions.
- It is a very unique story with human beings and animals who live on earth. On our planet, we multiply through "Mouda-Ja'ah" (Intercourse).
- On other planets, reproduction is done through different processes and methods; no physical contacts or sexual acts are necessary.
- Thus, there are no physical attachments, no corporal desire, and no sense of being physically possessed by another person, or committed to a physical partner.
- The collective mind of the community on some other planets substitutes for sexual desires, lust for the flesh, and corporal pleasures.
- Because humans can reach immortality in other dimensions starting in the Fifth dimension, freeing ourselves from physical memories is essential; this is done in the Fourth dimension.
- Once the purification is complete, and as soon as the process of freeing ourselves from past corporal memories is done, the Mind readjusts itself accordingly.
- This means, that almost everything we loved or treasured on earth, such as wealth, owning a luxurious car, properties, nice wardrobe, sexual pleasures, etc., become meaningless and shallow.
- This is why, we, the human beings…we are the lowest form of living entities in the universe, and our habitat "Ard" (Planet Earth) is lowest form of habitat in the universe. This decadence is caused by greed, violence, egoism, betrayal, and sexual bondage.

- Now, we go back to the deceased who is meeting the multiple spouses he/she had after the death of the first partner in life.
- The deceased will not feel embarrassed at all, because the Mind in the afterlife, once it has been purified, begins to understand that physical attachment causes sorrow and grief. And because there are no more sexual desires in the afterlife, these desires lose their meaning and importance.
- Consequently, the position of the deceased widow who is now pure Mind changes completely. Multiple spouses are no longer looked upon as multiple spouses, because they have acquired different nature and composition, and the association of the Mind with their physical properties on earth is integrated into the collective mind of the community.
- Thus, all of them will continue to live, think, and interact with each other as a continuous sequence of the chain of immortality free of physical attachment.

*** *** ***

61. Anunnaki's Device for Reading and Deciphering Codes and Symbols "Hazi-minzar", "Mnaizar"
⌘⌘⌘

I. Definition
II. Description
III. The text

I. Definition:
A small but sophisticated device used by the Ulema of the 8th degree to read and decipher codes and symbols from the Book of Ramadosh. It is composed of two words:
- **a**-Hazi, which means to read; to decipher a code.
- **b**-Minzar, which means an observation tool.

The word Mnaizar" is a diminutive of Minzar, referring to a smaller Minzar.

II. Description:
Ulema Mordechai gaves us a rare description of Hazi-minzar. His description appeared for the first time in the West in a book authored by Maximillien de Lafayette.

Here is an excerpt from his book:
The scene: Ulema Cheik Al Huseini talking to Germain Lumiere, a young Ulema, who is visiting the Cheik by invitation of Dr. Farid Tayara, a noted Ulema and head of a Masonic Lodge.
The place: Baalbeck, Lebanon, in the house of the Cheik.
The year: Around 1957-1958.

III. The text:
Germain Lumiere telling the story in his own words:

"Slowly, thoughtfully, I went to Dr. Farid's office, musing on all that has happened to me in the last few days; it was hard to digest. I was going to get instructions as to when and where I would be given the honor of reading *The Book of Rama Dosh*. Another miracle will manifest in my life.
Dr. Farid informed me that the arrangements have been made, and that the next day he would pick me up very early in the morning. We were to drive to Baalbeck, to see Cheik Al Huseini, my host during my previous trip to Baalbeck. It was there that I saw the startling printing of *The Book of Rama Dosh*, in the underground city. It would be nice to see him again. Dr. Farid added that Ulema Ghandahar, an expert on *The Book of Rama Dosh*, would join us at the Cheik's house.

The Cheik, as hospitable and pleasant as ever, was delighted to see me, and hugged me enthusiastically in the friendly and warm Arab fashion. "I knew you had the making of a great Ulema in you, Germain!" he said, holding me at arm's length and looking at my face with great affection. "You were such an attentive youth, and so fearless during our meeting with the Afrit, we were impressed!"
"I wish I had known you were impressed at the time," I said, laughing. "I felt like such a fool, and Taj made fun of me."
"Ah, that is just Taj," he said indulgently. "Such a silly man, like a big baby... But we all love him anyway. And he is doing very well now, with all the gold he got at the underground city."
"He was badly beaten for it by the Afrit," I said.
"You pay the price for everything in this world," said the Cheik philosophically. "But in the end, everything is as it should be. As we Arabs say, *Macktoob*! It is written... But come in, come in! Ulema Ghandahar is waiting for us in the library." My excitement at the thought of finally reading *The Book of Rama Dosh* hardly needs to be described.
We entered the house and went directly to the library. It was a much smaller room than I expected, and the pretty, carved and glassed over bookcases seemed to contain scholarly, but ordinary books, the kind you would find in any scholar's library.
I was surprised, since I expected a huge collection at Cheik Al Huseini's library. Little did I know what was to come...
The Cheik introduced me to Ulema Ghandahar, who shook my hand and said that he would be so happy to acquaint me with the most important book in the world.

Cheik Al Huseini went to one of the bookcases and pushed a hidden button among the carvings on the wood.

The case swerved to the side, and a short secret passage was revealed. We walked through it to a wooden door, and entered a library of immense proportions. The ceiling was very high, about fourteen feet in my estimate, and the room stretched to the proportions of a hall. Bookcases lined the walls, floor to ceiling, and more books were stacked on tables.

These books were mostly very old, as you could tell from the leather and cloth covers. However, not only books were there. Through the glassed doors on some of the cabinets I saw a huge collection of ancient rolled-up scrolls.

There was a divan on one side, and a few comfortable chairs, all done in the sumptuous Arab style. Diffused light came from the partially covered windows. This was exactly like the library I had imagined Cheik Al Huseini would have.

Of course, I thought. There are things here that should never be seen by the non-initiates. He must keep it secret.

Cheik Al Huseini went to one of the bookcases, looking for something, and without turning his head said, "Please, help yourselves!" I looked at the table before me, on which three cups of tea, which were not there a minute ago, suddenly materialized, accompanied by some pastries.

I smiled and looked at Dr. Farid, pointing silently at the tea cups. "This is only the beginning," he said mysteriously. My excitement mounted, I could not wait to see *The Book of Rama Dosh*, and I was wondering if that was what the Cheik was looking for. I sipped my tea and took a pastry.

It was interesting, I thought, how different the Ulema of the Middle East were from the Western ones, or the Chinese, even though their goals, aspirations, and ethics were exactly the same. For example, Rabbi Mordechai always said, "If you can do something normally, there is no reason to use the so-called supernatural powers."

Master Li was exactly the same.

I was taught the techniques that emphasized the power of mind, not techniques that had the touch of the magical.

The Middle Eastern Ulema did not think in those terms. They comfortably used all the magical techniques they wanted, and in addition, seemed to have contact with non-human entities who lived with them and worked for them.

I decided that the people of the Middle East loved emulating the sumptuous style of King Solomon, with his Afrit, gold, talking animals, flying carpets, and rivers of wine.

The Western Ulema tended to work like scientists, with a tendency toward austerity and a simple lifestyle. The differences were dictated by personality and culture, I suppose, because all of them wanted and achieved the same objectives, only reaching them by different roads.

The Cheik turned away from the book case, and walked a few feet toward us. He did not find the book he looked for, I thought, worried that it was lost and I will not be seeing it after all. A sense of disappointment went through me, but I noticed that the Cheik was doing something strange.

He turned toward the bookcase, lifted his arm, and pointed at the book case. Then he stopped, not moving. A second later, a book came floating toward him, and hovered in midair. The Cheik sat down and spoke a few words in a language that I did not know, but from the way he said it, I deduced that it was a code.

The book floated further toward him, and settled gently on the table. It was a big, heavy book, with a wood bark cover that had no marking on it to show what was its title.

The Cheik did not touch it. Instead, he went to a small table on the side of the divan, and brought a small box made of dark wood, inlaid with silver and mother of pearl. He put it next to the book.

"Germain, would you please go to the bathroom next door, take a shower, and put on the white robe that hangs on the door," the Cheik said. "We'll wait for you."

I did as I was told. While showering, I wondered if the book on the table was indeed *The Book of Rama Dosh*. How could it be? It looked quite different when the Cheik and Master Li printed it with the help of the Miraya plates and the light. Then, it looked like shining plastic, very modern, while the book on the library table was a normal, old book. Later I found out how this worked, so I might as well explain it right here.

The Book of Rama Dosh exists as only one copy. It is located in another dimension. Each time an Anunnaki-Ulema needs a copy, it must be printed directly from this original. Calling it requires special situations and techniques, such as I have seen in the underground city, but the advantage is, each copy is an exact facsimile of the original.

Other ancient books are subject to mistakes in printing, incorrect interpretation of words, etc., but not The Book of Ramadosh.

If this was the same copy that was printed in my presence, then the Cheik took the plates, which I remember him to wrap carefully in a silk scarf, to his own library, and there made sure it is properly wrapped in wood bark. It would never be wrapped in leather or any other animal-related substance. Of course, I could not be sure that this was the same copy, but no matter what, the content was always identical to the true, the one Book of Rama Dosh.

I put on the white robe, returned to the library and sat at the table with the other three. Cheik Al Huseini opened the book, so now I knew that must be The Book of Rama Dosh. I tried to keep calm. This would be the first time I would see Ana'kh printed in a book! And who could tell what the book is about?

The Cheik turned the page. It looked old. He turned a few other pages, each looking newer and smoother than the last. None of the pages had anything written on it, though. And yet, the three others seemed to be absorbed in reading the book!

Was I going mad?

I did not want to interrupt them, or ask questions, but I was beginning to feel desperate. Another page was turned, and it was again completely blank. I sighed with irritation. The Cheik suddenly stopped, looked at me and said, "*Moo Akhazaa*, forgive me, please."

He laughed gently. "You cannot see the writing without the necessary machine," he continued. "We no longer need it, at this stage, and when you get to stage 18 and over, you won't need it either, but for the moment, this machine will help you see the writing."

He opened the little box that was on the table next to the book, and took out a sophisticated-looking contraption.

It was obviously meant to be used as eyeglasses, but did not look like modern ones.

Rather, it was more like a Seventeenth Century Swiss watch, and I saw wheels attached to it on which certain letters and numbers were written, some big, some small, in an old and elegant font, looking like codes.

"What is this?" I asked. "It is going to help your vision," said Cheik Al Huseini. "Take a look at how it is constructed."

There were three layers of lenses for each eye, made of glass or crystal, completely transparent. A small wheel, made of gold and edged with green topaz, was attached to each lens, all on one side.

Each wheel had a little knob used for adjusting the codes. You would lift each lens individually, and adjust the wheel to the required code. On the other side was a larger wheel, about twice the size of the little wheels, and it adjusted itself to the position of the small wheels once they were in the perfect position.

Once the arrangement of the lenses and wheels was complete, the machine would allow you to see colors we usually do not see on earth.

Within these colors reside separate dimensions, or perhaps the colors reside in these dimensions, which is really one and the same. It is as if a door is opened to a spatial gate, an entrance to these parallel dimensions. You are on earth, but through your Conduit, you are entering an unearthly, separate dimension.

Now, put the machine on, and look at the bookcases. Don't look at the light from the window. This will allow your retina to adjust, and will bring up certain visual faculties."

"What does it do?" I asked, putting the machine on.

"It emulates the natural vision of the Anunnaki, who do not possess a retina, but a more complex mechanism. Even if you close your eyes, once you put the machine on, you can still see."

"What is the name of this machine?" I asked, still looking at the bookcase, as directed.

"It is called *Minaizar*, which is a diminutive of Minzar, the ability to see. The vision through the Minaizar is called *Nazra*," said the Cheik.

"I am seeing something strange," I said. "The bookcase is suddenly huge, astronomical..."

"But it is still visually very clear, right?" said the Cheik. "Unlike the usual type of visual enlargement, like a magnifier, which blurs everything and forces you to step back, the Minaizar retains its sharp image."

"This is true," I said, "But I feel a little dizzy..." I closed my eyes to refresh them, and was amazed that I could still see, just as the Cheik said before. I opened my eyes and returned to the table, sat down and looked at the book through the machine. Geometrical forms and numerical symbols were printed on the page I looked at. As I was gazing at them, they opened up, unfolded, and I saw letters coming through and appear on the page. Everything was written in pure, original Ana'kh. I could read *The Book of Rama Dosh*!

Here I must explain a few things about Ana'kh, which would clarify my reading. Ana'kh is a unique language, and has some characteristics that no earthly language possesses.

For example, when one wants to translate a page verbally from say, Latin to English, each person will have slight variations on the text that they will produce. The same would happen in simultaneous translation of any living language by a translator in the United Nations. Even when translating a book on paper the variations will appear, which is making translation more an art than a science. Not so with Ana'kh.

If a hundred Ulema will verbally translate a page written in Ana'kh, they will use the exact same words, in any language they use. The same goes for written translations. They are not really translating.

They are transmitting, rather, with the help of the Conduit, and no variations will ever occur.

Another interesting trait is that the phonetics make themselves clearly "heard" as you read Ana'kh, even if you have never seen or heard the word you are reading.

The words pronounce themselves for you, and no mistakes are ever made. The machine, of course, facilitates that, but it is accomplished by the Conduit. The machine is actually linked directly to the Conduit.

In any book, you cannot start in the middle of a paragraph or a word and still know what the page is all about. You must read a certain amount to grasp the meaning. With Ana'kh, each word presents its own meaning and message. There is no need for grammatical sequences.

The words, helped by the machine, follow you, rather than you follow them. In an ordinary book, you have to go back to certain pages if you want to retrace something. In Ana'kh, because of this tendency of the words to follow, you don't need to go back. Rather, you call the word to you.

The simplest analogy would be a search engine on a computer. You type the word on a search engine, and the connected messages appear. That is what happens with Ana'kh. When you look at a page, you encounter about three hundred *Nokta* – meaning spots, or messages. You look at a certain Nokta, and it opens up to thousands of other words and meanings.

The content is huge, but not intimidating, since it opens up in what seems to be multiple screens. Then, you can choose what you are interested in. I was reading along, finding it very easy to understand the pure, traditional Ana'kh, and completely comfortable with the viewing machine, so much so that I no longer noticed wearing it.

I was particularly interested in the creation of humanity, so the book took me to that moment in time. I kept doing this, moving from one Nokta to another, until I decided to move to another subject. I was fascinated by what the book had to offer regarding the dimensions and limitations of the universe.

I got the precise information I wanted regarding the question of whether the universe is expanding or shrinking. After that, I wandered into a Nokta regarding the future of humanity.

One thing led to another, and I was so totally absorbed, that I did not know if the other three were still with me or not, and certainly did not know how much time passed.

Finally, after watching millions of years enfold in front of me, I pulled back with a sigh. I felt the hand of Dr. Farid on my shoulder, and turned. "Do you know that you have been reading for two days?" he asked, smiling.

"Two days?" I asked, startled. "I did not eat, or drink, or sleep for two full days?"

"Yes," said Dr. Farid. "And you squeezed millions of years into two days. Time to go."

I did not feel it. Not a bit of exhaustion or thirst or hunger was caused by this intense study that lasted two days. On the contrary, I felt as comfortable and refreshed as if I came back from vacation. I mentioned that to Dr. Farid on our way back and he said that this was a common reaction, though some people did feel rather exhausted. Apparently it was an individual reaction. Still, he advised me to go to the hotel and rest."

*** *** ***

62. Entities Created by the Anunnaki, and the Ulema in Modern Times "Helama-Gooliim"
⌘ ⌘ ⌘

I. Definition and introduction
II. Their nature and essence
III. The creation process of these entities

I. Definition and introduction:
Name of entities (Human-like) created by Anunnaki-Ulema for the purpose of performing a good deed. They are part animal, part human, part Golem, part Ghoul; a hybrid race.
They are made of clay, or earth materials, much like all of us, but they have certain physical differences from both humans and animals.
They look exactly like normal people; they have eyes, hands, feet, etc. "They are not at all like machines or robots. You will not think them anything but human if you saw them..."said Ulema Mordechai.
They are born full adult. They are sensitive to light, so they work only by night, but they are nevertheless great engineers. Ulema Mordechai stated that when the Ulema, and some Kabbalists, reach the holy level of Kadash Daraja, they can create life. Real life.

II. Their nature and essence:
The creatures would function much like human beings, but they have three deep fundamental differences:
- 1-They don't have a soul,
- 2-They don't have a physical heart that functions like a blood pump,
- 3-They don't have a wired brain.

Their essence comes from another dimension, to which they return after their task is done. They are created for that task, and that is their only purpose. The creator tells them what to do, and they do it right away. In my case, I have created four of them to build houses for poor people in Estonia, and they did it very nicely, overnight."

III. The creation process of these entities:
Ulema Mordechai said: "I create each of them separately. For each, I bring with me seven pieces of papers on which I write certain codes, and I have to have my cane with me. Then I take soil, earth, or clay, and pour water on it to make it pliable. Once it's the right consistency, I mold it into a ball. I turn off most of the lights, leaving a very low illumination, maybe one candle or a small lamp, and pull back about four to five feet.

I then read a certain text that would encourage the ball to take the next step, which is to shape itself into an oblong of about four feet, and be ready to follow my special design. At that point I take my cane, walk to the other side of the oblong, dip the cane into the oblong, and stretch it.

I command the oblong to duplicate a human form, and it becomes a statue, lifeless, but similar in every way to the human form. I take the seven pieces of paper, and put two in the eyes, two in the ears, one in the mouth, and one on the breast, over the heart.

I roll the seventh piece as if it were a homemade cigarette, go to the other side of the statue, and throw the rolled paper at it. It always lands either in the nose or between the feet, and either position is correct.

The statue starts to move and attempts to stand up. At this time I turn around and leave the room for a few minutes, so as not to look at the statue as it comes to life. Seeing the actual transformation is forbidden by the Code of the Ulema, as stated in the Book of Rama Dosh.

I stand behind the door of the room, and wait until I hear the creature make a sound, which tells me that the procedure is complete.

I go back into the room, welcome the creature, give it clothes to wear, and pull out all the papers, to keep safely until such time as they are needed to disassemble the creature and send its essence back to its original dimension.

I create them to do one single task. When the task is accomplished, I ask them to lie on the floor, next to each other, return the pieces of paper with the codes to the correct places, and pour water over their bodies.

The bodies disappear, leaving earth on the floor, and the essence goes back to where it came from." Asking the Ulema: "Do they always go away peacefully?" he replied: "No, sometimes they develop a personality, if the task is a bit longer, and they have the delusion of being human and want to stay in our dimension. Of course it would be cruel and inhuman to let them stay, not to mention dangerous, but they do become tricky. So the Ulema or Kabbalist must be even trickier, and hypnotize the creature into deep sleep.

He then put the papers where they belong and set the paper on fire, and the body starts smouldering. At that time, we pour the water over them and they disappear...they built for me nice houses...The next morning, very early, I went to inspect the houses, and removed the great blanket that covered the area. The blanket is a large plasmic sheet that can create a shield of invisibility over the entire area. We just refer to it as a 'blanket' because it's a short and easy name..."

*** *** ***

63. Folding-Unfolding the Earth
"Hiraaba-safri"
⌘ ⌘ ⌘

Ulema Cheik Al Kabir explained:
Ulema Cheik Al Kabir explained this phenomenon. His exact words were: "Time is represented with two lines not perfectly aligned; one for you, the other for what is not you.

Space is represented with two circles, one for you, the other for what is not you. If you manage to place yourself between one of the two lines and one of the two circles without touching the other line and the other circle, you will conquer time-space.
Most people think, time goes straight from yesterday to tomorrow, through today, in one line, but they are wrong, and great thinkers understand the malleability of time and space.
Sufis, Gnostics, pre-Islamic, Islamic, and Jewish scholars, all wrote about it.
The Jewish Kabbalists, in particular, engaged themselves in the study of Tay Al Ard, but had a different name for it, in Hebrew. They called it Kefitzat Haderach, meaning, word by word, 'the jumping of the road,' but translated as the ability to jump instantaneously from one place to another or travel with unnatural speed.
It was widely documented by them.

*** *** ***

64. Longevity of Quasi-Human-Life Form "Izra-nafar-mikla'ch"
⌘⌘⌘

I. Definition
II. The Anunnaki-Ulema explains

I. Definition:
A term referring to the longevity of quasi-human-life form, such as Golem and hybrids. The term is explained in a Q&A from one of the Anunnaki-Ulema Kira'ats (Reading and lectures).

II. The Anunnaki-Ulema explain:
A student asked: Can hybrids reach immortality through genetic manipulations?

Answer of the honorable Ulema:
- Although hybrids are intelligent beings, they should not to be considered neither humans nor extraterrestrials.
- Their essence (DNA) is not pure.
- They are genetically created either by human beings, or by a malicious extraterrestrial race.
- Any living creature Dha-kiliyan (Genetically) created by humans will never reach immortality.
- Because a Dha-kiliyi (Genetic) creation of other living-forms manufactured by human beings is an artificial product, this Dha-kiliyi (Genetic) product which does not include the first energy element introduced in regular human beings by the Anunnaki will totally disintegrate without leaving the "Shou'la" (Spark of life).

- The Shou' la was created on earth by the Anunnaki. No human ever succeeded in duplicating a Shou'la.
- Any living creature Dha-kiliyan (Genetically) created on earth or in other physical dimensions by a malicious extraterrestrial race coming from a lower dimension will not reach immortality.

Authors' note: We do believe that the honorable Ulema was referring to what American ufologists call the "Greys", even though, he has never used the word "Greys".
It is our belief that this word is an American ufology terminology. The word he used was "Min Kariji al-dounia".
Min means from.
Kariji means outside or outer.
Dounia means the world.

- Living entities created by the Greys (A lower intraterrestrial alien race) are born contaminated.
- The Greys' contamination prevents these living entities (Hybrids, half humans-half-extraterrestrials) from ascending to the Ba'ab.
- Consequently, the hybrids will not enter the other dimensions and reach immortality.

*** *** ***

65. Immortality After Death "Izrahi-ghafra"
⌘⌘⌘

I. Definition
II. The Anunnaki-Ulema explains

I. Definition:
A term related to the concept and/or Anunnaki-Ulema's thoughts on various states of metamorphosis of the mind-body of a deceased in the after-life. The concept is herewith explained in a Q&A from one of the Ulema's Kira'ats (Readings and lectures).

II. The Anunnaki-Ulema explain:
A student asked the Ulema: Do we become immortal if we follow the teachings of the Ulema?
Answer of the honorable Ulema:
- On earth, humans cannot reach immortality. Afterlife, the "Tahirin" (Purified ones) will reach immortality.
- But we have to understand what immortality is?
- Is it an eternal existence?
- What kind of existence? Is it physical or spiritual?
- Mental or organic? Terrestrial or extraterrestrial?
- Nothing in the universe lasts for ever, not even the universe itself. Despite the fact that the universe is expanding, it will eventually cease to exist.

Authors' note: Contemporary leading scientists in the field of cosmology and quantum physics agree with the honorable Ulema. They have publicly stated, that soon or later, the universe will cease to exist. Those who believe in Jesus, Mohammad, Krishna, Vishnu, Jehovah, and Allah don't.

- It is very important to keep in mind, that so many extraterrestrial beings came to earth, thousands of years

ago. We are aware of 46 different alien races who have visited planet earth.
- Some of these alien races created early forms of human beings. I say forms, because at the time these living creatures were created by the aliens, they lacked mental faculties. Some looked like us, but not exactly.
- We know from the manuscripts of Melkart and the "Society of the Fish" which was established by the early Phoenicians who lived on the Island of Arwad, that the primitive human beings were called "Intelligent animals" because they behaved and lived like animals, but were more intelligent than the beasts of the earth.
- These beings were created by extraterrestrials who came from a lower dimension, even though, they were highly advanced. The extraterrestrials did not install a Conduit in the brain cells of the primitive beings.
- Without a Conduit, no living creature can ascend to the Madkhal or Ba'ab. Consequently, a passage to the Fourth dimension is virtually impossible without a Conduit.
- These primitive creatures did not reach immortality, because they did not go through the Ba'ab. Because they did not have a mind, but brain's membranes, they were unable to continue to live afterlife.
- In the afterlife, you continue to live only with your mind.
- Your mind is the source of energy that keeps you alive.
- The primitive creatures did not have a mind, although their brain was wired like an electronic machine. Their brain was not developed at all, and as a result, their race became extinct.
- They perished, not because of famine, wars, or fall of asteroids on earth, but because of the deterioration of the cells of their brains.
- You will not find these primitive creatures on other planets, or in parallel dimensions.
- Humans who were "Dha-kiliyan" (Genetically) created by the Anunnaki will eventually reach immortality, as long as the universe remains in existence.
- The early living-forms of humans, primitive creatures, intelligent animals, and monstrous robotic human-like species vanished from the face of the earth some 65,000-61,000 years ago.

- When the Igigi came to planet earth, some 65,000 years ago, they captured many of those primitive half human, half animal creatures who were living in Australia, Madagascar, Brazil, Indonesia, Central Africa and some regions of Europe, and transformed them Dha-kiliyan (Genetically) into an upgraded form of humans. Still, they looked like robotic animals. A few years later, they died out.
- Some 65,000-60,000 years ago, three extraterrestrial races Dha-kiliyan (Genetically) created a new human race.
- They were the Lyrans, the Nordics, and the Anunnaki. The newly created human race had a mind (Not to be confused with soul), brains' cells and a dormant Conduit.
- Because a Conduit was installed in their brains, our ancestors were destined to reach immortality. Today, we are the offspring and descendants of the intelligent human race created by these three extraterrestrial races.
- Yes, you can say, the Anunnaki made us immortals.

*** *** ***

66. Columns "charged" with Anunnaki's Supernatural Powers "Jachim", "Jachin"
⌘ ⌘ ⌘

Two large cast-bronze pillars in the Temple of Solomon.
Ana'kh/Ulemite/Hebrew. Noun.
Pronounced Ya-chim in Ana'kh.
I. Definition and introduction
III. Ulema's interpretation

I. Definition and introduction:
Jachin and Boaz were the names given by the Phoenician builder and architect Huram "Hiram" to two large cast-bronze pillars that stood on either side of the entrance to the Temple in Jerusalem, also called the Temple of Solomon. Huram was also the architect of the Temple.
Jachin and Boaz were immense, impressive in design and architectural structure; eighteen cubits (about 27 feet) high and twelve cubits (about 18 feet) around, and were decorated with secret symbolic Phoenician motifs.

II. Ulema's interpretation:
Ulemite literature suggests that the Jachin and Boaz were columns "charged" with Anunnaki's supernatural powers.
The Two Pillars called "Amid" in Phoenician and Ana'kh (Plural of Amud, which means a column in Phoenician, Ugaritic, and Arabic) appear to play a paramount role on the landscape of esoteric knowledge, as elaborately depicted in the Anunnaki-Ulema extraterrestrial manuscript, the "Book of Ramadosh".

Ulema Naphtali ben Yacob said, verbatim, "The two pillars were an architectural structure in the Temple of Solomon, but the fact that they were unattached to the floor's foundation, and stood as a composition of free-standing columns reveals their esoteric-metaphysical importance in Ana'kh literature.
The Amid "Two Pillars" have a deep meaning, known only to the "Illuminated".

The Amid (Pillars; columns) are a primordial, and an integral part of the Eluhi Matrix (Divine Grid; Creator's Plan), which defines the very structure and nature of the multiple existences of the physical and non-physical beings, who inhabit our world, and commonly reffered to, and/or called the Elohim, Nafar, the extraterrestrials, intraterrestrials, hybrids, and humans

The Two Pillars represent many things, and are traditionally related to and associated with (To name a few):

- 1-Duality of Man;
- 2-Molecular copies of mankind;
- 3-Trans-Teleportation;
- 4-Metal transmutation;
- 5-Solomon's gold mine;
- 6-The Knights Templar;
- 7-St. John of Malta Order;
- 8-Electro-magnetic mind-body Saphra (Entering-Exiting adjacent non-physical dimension);
- 9-Hiram-Solomon Freemasonry Brotherhood;
- 10-The Atlantean pillars/gates;
- 11-The origin of religions.

*** *** ***

67. Abbreviation of Yahweh "Jah", "Yah"
⌘ ⌘ ⌘

Phoenician/Ana'kh/Ulemite/Hebrew. Noun.
I. Definition
II. In Ana'kh/Ulemite literature

I. Definition:
Jah "Yah" is an abbreviation of Jehovah.
It is derived from the Ana'kh word Ha-yah, which means life.
In Hebrew, it **means,** to be, come to pass.
The ultimate name is the Divine Name Jah; the name-title of the Creator, the chief of the angels (Called Supreme Beings, the Gods, and/or Extraterrestrial Anunnaki-Nephilim.)

II. In Ana'kh/Ulemite literature:
In Ana'kh/Ulemite literature, Jah also means, the galactic source of all living beings. In other words, the primordial cosmic life-being in the whole universe, and its multiple dimensions.
Yah "Jah" is also one of the creators of the Anunnaki.
Ulema Stanbouli said verbatim, "The world is not a divine creation that happened in six days, as described in the Bible, and the Scriptures. Our world was created outside the landscape and perimeter of the physically measurable cosmos.
What we see on Earth, in our skies, heavens, planets, and galaxies, stars, and far beyond what we can see, originated in another dimension, and this other dimension also originated from another one.
Some of the copies of the universe, including ours, our Earth, and ourselves were created according to non-physical blueprints of many "Supreme Architects", who existed in other planes, billions of years, before God's name and existence were invented

by humans, whether in their imagination, in caves, in temples, or epics.

These creators were the Jah." Ulema Stanbouli said verbatim, "The world is not a divine creation that happened in six days, as described in the Bible, and the Scriptures. Our world was created outside the landscape and perimeter of the physically measurable cosmos. What we see here on planet Earth, in our skies, heavens, planets, galaxies, stars, and far beyond what we can see or we would see, originated in another dimension, and this other dimension also originated from another one.

Some of the copies of the universe, including ours, our Earth, and ourselves were created according to non-physical blueprints of many "Supreme Architects", who existed in other planes, billions of years, before God's name and existence were invented by humans, whether in their imagination, in caves, in temples, or epics.

These creators were the Jah.

Ulema Naphtali said verbatim, "Humans were not created in the image of God. We were created genetically from Turab, an Earth's substance and the DNA of an advanced extraterrestrial race called Annaki or Al Anna'kh.

And the Annaki were "fashioned" according to Jah's specific formula.

Parts of this formula are:
- **a**-Rouhiyya, meaning etheric;
- **b**-Sham-kiya, meaning cosmic (Cosmic dust and molecules); and
- **c**-Birza, which means mental projection...The Jah, plural or singular, male of female, or non male and non female were the architects and geneticists of the formula of life, the cosmos, and time-space concept."

*** *** ***

68. Anunnaki's Sex and Reproduction "Jin.Si-Yah"
⌘ ⌘ ⌘

I. Introduction
II. Hybrids
III. Major points about the subject

I. Introduction:
Ulema Maximillien de Lafayette said, "In the Anunnaki's society, sex and reproduction are two separate functions. Anunnaki reproduction is done by technology, involving the light passing through the woman's body until it reaches her ovaries and fertilizes her eggs.
The eggs go into a tube. The woman is lying on a white table for this procedure, surrounded by female medical personnel. If performed by uncaring aliens (such as the grays and the reptilians) it is unpleasant and even can be painful, which has given rise to the abductee's stories of suffering.
However, not all aliens are created equal.
The Anunnaki, which are a very compassionate race, are very gentle and the procedure is harmless. Apparently, the Anunnaki version of sex is much more enjoyable for both genders.
It involves an emanation of light from both participants. The light mingles and the result is a joy that is at the same time physical and spiritual. The Anunnaki do not have genitals the way we do.

II. Hybrids:
As a hybrid becomes more and more Anunnaki, he/she loses the sexual organs and becomes physically like the Anunnaki.
The hybrid welcomes the changes and feels that he/she has gained a lot through the transformation. The Anunnaki mate for life, like ducks.

They don't even understand the concept of infidelity, and don't have a word for cheating, mistress, extramarital affairs, etc. in their language.

Like many extraterrestrials, the Anunnaki do not have genital organs, but a lower level of aliens who inhabit the lowest interdimensional zone and aliens-hybrids living on earth do. The stories of the abductees who claim to have had sex with Anunnaki are to be disregarded. Those stories are pure fiction.

III. Major points about the subject:
- **1**-Aliens reproduce in laboratories.
- **2**-Aliens do not practice sex at all.
- **3**-Aliens fertilize "each other" and keep the molecules (not eggs or sperms, or mixed liquids from males and females) in containers at a very specific temperature and following well defined fertilization reproduction specs.
- **4**-Alien babies are retrieved from the containers after 6 months.
- **5**-The following month, the mother begins to assume her duty as a mother. Alien mothers do not breast-feed their babies, because they do not have breast, nor do they produce milk to feed their babies.
- **6**-Alien babies are nourished by a "light conduit."
- **7**-Human sperm or eggs are useless to extraterrestrials of the higher dimension.
- **8**-Extraterrestrials are extremely advanced in technology and medicine. Consequently, they do NOT need any part, organ, liquid or cell from the human body to create their own babies. However, there are aliens who live in lower dimensions and zones who did operate on abductees for other reasons – some are genetic, others pure experimental."

*** *** ***

69. Short Mental Projection of the Self "Ka"
⌘ ⌘ ⌘

I. Definition
II. Ka and the Egyptians

I. Definition:
A short mental projection of the "Self". In Ana'kh literature, "Self" is interpreted in numerous ways.
For instance:
- **a-** Ka is one of the many holographic images of one's thoughts. Meaning, that all thoughts, ideas and feelings can materialize quasi-physically. Ideas and inner feelings have frequencies and particular colors, visible to the enlightened ones. Seeing these holographic images is a process that can be learned and mastered, following an Ulema's orientation program.
- **b-** Ka is the materialized form/shape of one's original copy, meaning the primordial substance and/or structure of a physical body. At first, a person is conceived as a non-physical substance, a sort of an idea, a creation's blueprint.
- **c-** Following various stages, Ka takes definition in a human-body shape, according to a prescribed design. This design contains everything that will play major role in one's life, encompassing health, wealth, success, failure, luck, intelligence, etc.
- **d-** Ka is also is the mirrored image of one's double.

II. Ka and the Egyptians:
The Secret Doctrine explained that "The Egyptians were familiar with this concept. The Egyptian Ka is the equivalent to the astral

double, model-body, or linga-sarira. The ancient Egyptians held that when a human being was born, the ka was born with him and remained with him throughout his life."

*** *** ***

70. Multiple Dimensions' Dividing Lines "Kalem"
⌘⌘⌘

Lines or graphs referred to as the invisible borders of multiple adjacent zones of existences, also called multiple dimensions, and/or parallel universes.

These lines serve also as a path or a passage that lead to a higher sphere of knowledge. From Kalem, derived the Hebrew word Kailem, which literally means, vessels or vehicles; the vases for the source of the Waters of Life, used in the Ten Sephiroth, and considered as the primeval *nuclei* of all Kosmic Forces.

Some Kabalists and occultists stated that these lines or vessels appear in our world, through twenty two canals, which are represented by the twenty-two letters of the Hebrew alphabet, "thus making with the Ten Sephiroth thirty-two paths of wisdom."

According to Anunnaki-Ulema Li, "The world of humans is linked to the afterlife through twenty two Kalem (Graphs). Some of these graphs or lines are directly attached to the "Conduit" implanted in the human brain, thus a trained adept can enter and exist other dimensions by placing himself or herself on one of the "tracks" of these lines."

*** *** ***

71. Center of Energy "Kama"
⌘ ⌘ ⌘

I. Definition
II. In Hebrew, esoterica and Kabala

I. Definition:
Called "a center of energy", by Ulema Oppenheimer.
Also referred to as the "Manifestation Square", meaning a zone where different forms of appearances, including beings and higher entities manifest themselves for multiple reasons.
The Manifestation Square is indeed a physical area on Earth. Some Ulema suggested that this Square serves as a platform for the Ba'ab.

According to Ulema Stanbouli, the Earth is full of these Squares. However, they are not permanent, meaning they appear on Earth, each time a cosmic molecule or "Buble" collides with another Bubble. This happens cosmically.

In one of his Kiraat, Ulema Maximillien de Lafayette said, "The Manifestation Squares materialize on Earth, when two distinct yet very close dimension membranes "bump" into each other. Ulema Stanbouli added, "The whole universe was created in this way."

II. In Hebrew, esoterica and Kabala:
From Kama, derived the Hebrew word Kamea, which means a magic square. In esoterica and occult studies, Kama or Kamea are a place, or a zone used by Kabalists and occultists to communicate with non-human entities in order to accomplish magical acts.

73. Etheric Manifestation "Karsha-bita"
⌘ ⌘ ⌘

I. Definition
II. The bird as a symbol of the soul

I. Definition:
An orb; an etheric manifestation, sometime referred to as one aspect of the mind; others use the word "Soul" instead of mind. In a passage from the Book of Ramadosh, Karsha-bita was described the lower level of the Mind (Soul), equated with physical desires and ego.

II. The bird as a symbol of the soul:
E. Erickson stated that "The Persian word Karshipta derived from Karsha-bita, for it reflects a striking similarity.
For instance, the Persian Karshipta in the Mazdean Scriptures means the holy bird of Heaven, of which Ahura Mazda says to Zaratushta that "he recites the Avesta in the language of birds." The bird is the symbol of "Soul" of Angel and Deva in every old religion.
It is easy to see, therefore, that this "holy bird" means the divine Ego of man, or the Soul".

*** *** ***

73. Hybrids' Dwellings
"Korashag"
"Khur-Shag"
⌘⌘⌘

I. Definition and introduction
II. Description of the hybrids' habitat
a- Human environment
b- Underground/underwater communities
III. Characteristics
Bedrooms, beds, toys, dining rooms, food, and eating habits
IV. Hybrid children habitat as described by an Anunnaki
a. Inside the base
b. The refectory
c. Hybrids' three distinct groups/categories
d. Hybrids placed for adoption
e. Disposing of the food and cleaning the refectory
f. Dormitories and sleeping quarters
g. Attending various activities
h. The fetuses' room

Dwellings
"Korashag"
"Khur-Shag"
⌘⌘⌘

I. Definition and introduction
II. Description of the hybrids' habitat
a- Human environment
b- Underground/underwater communities
III. Characteristics
Bedrooms, beds, toys, dining rooms, food, and eating habits
IV. Hybrid children habitat as described by an Anunnaki
a. Inside the base
b. The refectory
c. Hybrids' three distinct groups/categories
d. Hybrids placed for adoption
e. Disposing of the food and cleaning the refectory
f. Dormitories and sleeping quarters
g. Attending various activities
h. The fetuses' room

I. Definition and introduction:
Korashag "Khur-Sha" is an Anunnaki/Ulemite word for a hybrids' habitat. The hybrid-human race is very different from hybrid extraterrestrial race living on other planets. The hybrid-humans look exactly like human beings, but are much shorter, and have different facial structure.

II. Description of the hybrids' habitat:
Ulema Maximillien de Lafayette said: These hybrid children live in two different ways.

- **a- Human environment:**

The first is the human environment. This happens when a hybrid child had been adopted by a human family, usually, by a high ranking United States military man working with aliens in secret military underground bases.

This top echelon military man adopts a hybrid child and raises him or her as a human being. This happens much more often than most people imagine.

- **b- Underground/underwater communities:**

The second kind of habitat is a large communal living in underground and/ or underwater dormitories, or sometimes in above ground level dormitories, but always on Earth.

III. Characteristics:
Bedrooms, beds, toys, dining rooms, food, and eating habits.

- **1.** While the adult hybrid usually has his or her own room, the children live together.
- **2.** Their dormitories are like a combination of old fashioned orphanages, and military barracks.
- **3.** The rooms don't have high ceilings, rarely over twelve feet, they are extremely long, and they have no windows.
- **4.** The rooms are spotlessly clean; they are cleaned constantly by a vacuum system that sucks away all dirt.
- **5.** They have no need of trash cans.
- **6.** The colors of the rooms are sad, nothing appealing about them, dark, and basically gray metallic color.
- **7.** The beds are arranged on top of each other, like in a submarine. There are no ladders reaching the higher level beds, since the children can levitate. For each dormitory, there are dozens and dozens of three beds row sections.
- **8.** These beds are assembled like prefab furniture, quickly and efficiently. The materials the beds are built from are very different from any material used in standard furniture. It is a kind of metal, very smooth, and of silver-gray color. For the second and third levels, parts of the bed are magnetic, so the children can attach their toys to it.

- **9.** On the first level, the toys are around the bed. They are given a choice of toys because the Grays believe the toys would be part of their education and adjustment.
- **10.** If a child wishes to hide his or her toys, the bed can be closed and pushed into the wall. For their bathroom needs, they go to an adjacent room, also communal, where baths and toilets are available to them.
- **11.** Cleanliness is scrupulously maintained there as well as in the dormitory. The children eat in refectories.
- **12.** These dining rooms are long, and contain extremely long tables. The food is served from within the table, which opens up at the outside edge of the table and reveals the plates.
- **13.** When they finish eating, the plates, which are metal, are left on the table. The table absorbs the plate and sends it to the dishwasher. Despite all the precautions and the cleanliness, many children die from various diseases and never reach adulthood.
- **14.** When a child dies, he or she is cremated.
- **15.** The Grays refer to it as "incineration."

III. Hybrid children habitat as described by an Anunnaki:

The following is an actual depiction of their habitat acoording to Sinhar Ambar Anati, the Phoenician-American hybrid woman, known to us as Victoria. She is married to SinharMarduck, an Anunnaki leader.
Victoria (Ambar Anati) is conversing with her mother-in-law, Sinharinannaschamra who is the mother of SinharMarduck. Here is the text (Title; Visiting the Hybrids):

a. Inside the base:

Sinharinannaschamra said: "The base we are going to visit is an underwater habitat. We are about to descend way down into the Pacific.""What about air?" I asked, a bit apprehensive about the idea. Surely She won't forget I could not breathe under water, but still..."We pass through a lock that is safe for water and air," said Sinharinannaschamra, "and inside, it's geared for the hybrids, which, just like humans, need air."

In a few minutes, we stopped and I assumed, correctly, that we were already inside the base. "They are expecting us," she said. "Don't worry about them. They know I can blow the whole place up if they dare to give me any trouble."

The spaceship's door opened and I saw that we were inside a huge, hangar-like room. If I had expected a beautiful, aquarium-like window, showing the denizens of the deep playing in their blue environment, I would have been disappointed. But knowing the Grays, I expected nothing of the sort, and so the beige and gray room, all metal and lacking any windows, did not exactly surprise me.

"This base is enormous," said Sinharinannaschamra. "It is used for many operations, but we will just concentrate on the hybrids today."

I was pleased to hear that, since I was secretly apprehensive about the possibility of stumbling on one of the Grays' hellish laboratories. I will never forget, or forgive, what I saw in their lab. But I said nothing and waited to see what was to happen next. Sinharinannaschamra walked me to a solid wall, put her hand on it, and wall shimmered a little and then moved, allowing a door to form and open for us.

b. The refectory:

We entered a long corridor, illuminated by stark, white light, with many regular doors on each side. Sinharinannaschamra opened one of the doors and we entered a large room, obviously a refectory since it contained extremely long tables, all made of metal. The room was painted entirely in beige – tables, chairs, walls, and ceiling, and had no windows. It was scrupulously clean. Suddenly, the tables opened up, each table revealing a deep groove on each of its long sides.

Plates of what seemed to be normal human food were released from the grooves, and placed each before a chair. At this moment, a few doors opened at various parts of the room, and from each door an orderly file of children came in and settled at the table.

They were completely silent, not a word was heard, as they picked up their forks and began to eat. None of them paid any attention to us, even though we stood at plain view. The children seemed to range from six to twelve, but it was difficult to be sure of that. On one hand, they were small and fragile, so I might have mistaken their ages.

On the other hand, their eyes gave the impression of almost old age. They seemed wise beyond their tender years. Their hair was thin, their skin was pale to gray, and they all wore white clothes of extreme cleanliness.

c. Hybrids' three distinct groups/categories:
Despite these similarities, which made them look as if they were all related to each other, I could tell some differences between them that seemed rather fundamental. It was almost as if they fitted within three distinct groups. I mentioned it, in a whisper, to Sinharinannaschamra, and she nodded. "Yes, you got it," she said. "They consist of early-stage hybrids, middle-stage hybrids, and late-stage hybrids.

- **1**-The first group is born from the first combination of abductees' and Grays' DNA. They closely resemble the Grays. Look at their skin – the grayish color is very close to that of the Grays, and so is the facial structure.
- **2**-The second group, the middle-stage hybrids, are the result of mating between these early-stage ones, once they are old enough for reproduction, and human abductees. The resulting DNA is closer to humans, and so they look much more like humans, and many of them lose the Progeria gene.
- **3**-The third group, the late-stage hybrid, is the most important. Middle-stage hybrids are mated with humans to create them – and they can hardly be distinguished from humans." "Yes, I can tell who the late-stagers are quite easily," I said.

d. Hybrids placed for adoption:
"But there are not too many of them here, right?" "This is true, not too many are here. A large number of these hybrids, who represent the most successful results of the experiments, are placed for adoption with human families."

"Are the human families aware of the origin of their children?"
"Yes, in most cases they are. Generally, they are adopted by a high-ranking United States military man or woman, who had worked, or still works, with aliens, in secret military bases. This happens much more often than most people suspect... the spouse of the military person may or may not know, depending on

circumstances and character traits. These lucky hybrids lead a much better life than whose who are raised in places like this one, communally."

"Are they badly treated here? Are they abused by the Grays?"

"No, the Grays don't want to lose them, they are too valuable. But they receive no love, no individual attention, there is no real parenting, and the environment is barren and depressing. They live like that until they are old enough to be of use in the experiments. Not a very nice life for any child."

"And what about Progeria? I mean, for the adopted ones."

"Only the hybrids who are entirely free of Progeria are adopted by human families. We even suspect, though we are not sure, that many of the Progeria stricken late-stagers are killed, since their Progeria gene is too strong. The Grays believe that after these three attempts, it cannot be eradicated by further breeding."

"And so they kill the poor things... what is the motive for all these atrocities?"

"All for the same reason I have mentioned. They think they somehow will save their civilization. But they are doomed."

"But in the meantime, they harm, torture, and kill so many people.
I don't understand why it is tolerated." Sinharinannaschamra did not answer.

e. Disposing of the food and cleaning the refectory:

The children finished eating, still in complete silence. Each child, as he or she finished his meal, leaned back into the chair, and as soon as all of them were leaning back, the groove from which the plates came opened up, and re-absorbed all the plates.

"They now go to an automatic dishwashing machine," explained Sinharinannaschamra.

The children got up, and left the dismal room in the same file arrangement they came in. As soon as the room was empty, large vacuum cleaners emerged from the wall and sucked up every crumb, every piece of debris.

Then they sprayed the tables and floor with a liquid that smelled like a disinfectant. The room was spotlessly clean again, ready for the next sad, depressing meal.

f. Dormitories and sleeping quarters:

"Shall we go to the dormitories now?"
Asked Sinharinannaschamra. I nodded.
We followed the children through one of the doors, and entered a place that was a combination of an old-fashioned orphanage and military barracks.
It was a very large room, but the ceiling was not high, only about twelve feet. Again, everything was beige and gray, and there were no windows to relieve the monotony.
The room was full of beds, arranged above each other in groups of three, like in a submarine. Dozens and dozens of such rows seemed to stretch to a very long distance.
The beds were made of some metal, very smooth, and of silver-gray color. They seemed to be assembled like prefab furniture.
"Sinharinannaschamra," I said, "there are no ladders. How do the children reach the upper levels?"
"They can levitate," said Sinharinannaschamra.
"Look at this. Part of each bed is magnetic, so each child can have his or her toys attach to it. As for the lower beds, the toys are stored next to them."
"So they have toys," I said.
"That's a mercy."
"Yes, the Grays discovered that mental stimulation is highly important to the hybrids' development. There are plenty of other activities, mostly with abductees, that relieve their lives of the tedium, at least to a certain extent."
"But they have no privacy at all."
"None whatsoever, they only get their own room when they are more mature, but they have one thing that pleases them. If the children want to, they can put their things in their bed, close the bed with a panel, and hide it inside a wall. They like that."
"I wonder, too, if it is not a comfort for them to be together, after all."
"Their feelings and emotional climate are not exactly human...it's hard to explain.
I think it's time for you to see them interact."
"Where are all the children now?" "They are attending various activities," said Sinharinannaschamra.
"Come, I'll show you."

g. Attending various activities:

We entered a room that opened directly from the dormitory. To my surprise, it was really a glass bubble. You could see the outside, which was an unpleasant desert surrounding. I found it nasty, but I figured that to the children it might have represented a pleasant change. About ten children, seemingly between the ages of six and eight, sat on the ground, which was simply the desert sand. They were playing with normal human toys – trucks, cars, and trains.
They filled the things with sand, using plastic trowels that one usually sees on the beach. They were also building tunnels from the sand, wetting it with water from large containers that stood here and there.
They seemed to be enjoying their games, certainly concentrating on them, but their demeanor remained quiet and subdued, and they did not engage in the laughter, screaming, yelling, or fighting that children of this age usually produce.
"They also have rooms with climbing equipment, and places to play ball," said Sinharinannaschamra.
"It is needed to strengthen their bones and muscles," she added.

I approached the children, a little apprehensively, worrying that I might frighten the poor things. They looked up at me, seemingly waiting for me to do something, but I was pleased to realize that they were not afraid.
I sat on the sand, took some stones that were scattered around, and arranged them so that they created a little road. The children stared at me for a minute with their strange, wise eyes, as if trying to read my thoughts, and almost instantly grasped the idea and continued to build the road together. None of them smiled, but they seemed very much engaged in the new activity. Once all the stones were used, they looked at me again, as if trying to absorb information, and sure enough, after a minute they took the trucks and make them travel on the little road. I got up and let them play.
"So they read minds," I said to Sinharinannaschamra.
"To an extent," she said. "At this age, they basically just absorb images you project. You probably thought about the trucks going on this road, and they saw it..." and she added. "And everything was done together, as if they were mentally connected,"
I asked: "Do they do everything together?"
"Yes, everything is communal, even the bathrooms where they clean themselves. But don't be too upset about it. If they are

separated from each other before their adolescence, they are extremely upset. It is almost as if the onset of puberty makes them an individual, and before that they have a group mentality."
"Horrible," I said.
"They are not unhappy," said Sinharinannaschamra.
"Only as adolescents, when they break off the communal mind, they understand how unhappy they are. But we will visit the adolescents on another occasion."
"Very well," I said.

h. The fetuses' room:
Sinharinannaschamra asked: "Would you like to see the room where they keep the fetuses?" I followed her to the corridor, and we walked quite a distance before opening another door.
We entered another one of the hangar-sized rooms, full of tanks. "Each tank contains colored and different liquid nutrients," said Sinharinannaschamra.
"This is where they put the fetuses, as soon as they are removed from the abductees. The tanks are arranged in order, from the youngest fetuses to those that are almost ready to be removed."
"Do they separate them into their stages?" I asked.
"Yes, this room is for early stagers only. In other rooms, they have the middle stagers. But the late stagers remain in the mother's womb until birth, to make them as close to humans as possible."
"And what are the babies like?"
"Quiet, not as responsive as human babies. Many of them die as soon as they are removed from the tank. Those that survive are generally mentally well developed, physically weak, and emotionally subdued."
"And who takes care of them?"
"Both the Grays and the abductees. The Grays perform most of the physical requirements, but the abductees supply the human touch. We can't go there yet."
"How come?"
"We need to prepare you to interact with abductees. They are very complicated. We shall have a few sessions about interacting with them at the same time we teach you how to work with the adolescents. Also, you wanted some instructions of how to contact and help those people that are children of humans and Anunnaki, like your son. This should take some teaching, too."

We went back to our spaceship, not saying much. I remember thinking that if I were part of the Anunnaki Council, I would vote to kill every Gray in the known universe. Of course I did not say it to Sinharinannaschamra, but I am sure she knew how I felt. Back home, I went to my beloved garden and sat under a tree that constantly showered tiny blossoms on me, like little snowflakes. I did not even know I was crying.

"What is the matter?" said Marduchk, who suddenly appeared next to me. I told him about the visit with the hybrids.

"The hybrids are not abused," said Marduchk.

"Something else is bothering you." I thought for a moment, and then decided I might as well be honest with him. "Yes," I said.

"I cannot understand the Anunnaki's casual attitude about the fact that thousands of human beings are tortured and killed all the time. Neither you nor Sinharinannaschamra seem to be as shocked as I am about the fact that the Grays engage in such atrocities." Marduchk was quiet for a minute, thinking. At this conversation, we did not use the Conduit, because at my agitated state I found it difficult. I was not entirely used to it as yet. So I waited for him to say what he thought. "I see your point," he said. "You think we are callous about it."

"Yes, I do, to tell you the truth. Why don't you destroy the Grays? Why do you allow so much death, so much pain? Are you, after all, cruel beings? Have you become callous because you have lived so many years, and became thick-skinned about suffering?"

"No, we are not cruel. It's just that we view life and death differently than you do. We cannot destroy all the Grays, even if we wanted to. We don't commit genocide, even if they try to do it. But we don't want to kill them. We know that they will die on their own." "And in the meantime, suffering means nothing to you?" "It means a lot, but destroying the Grays would not eliminate suffering in all the universes we go to. There are other species that are even worse, you just don't know them because the objects of their behavior are not humans."

"It seems to me, that even though you are so much more sophisticated than the humans, the fact that you deny the existence of God may have deprived you of your ethics, after all."

"Deny God? What makes you think we deny God?" asked Marduchk. He seemed genuinely surprised. "Marduchk, you have told me, more than once, that the Anunnaki created the human race, not God. So where is God if He is not the Creator? Your statements are contradictory."

74. Physical manifestation of a dead person, before entering another dimension
"Kusir and Lalladu"
⌘ ⌘ ⌘

1. Introduction
2. Kusir and Lalladu
a. Meaning of Kusir
Kusir-Ra
Kusir-Ji
b. Meaning of Lalladu

---

1. Introduction:
Ulema Lafayette said, "Quite often, students and readers alike, ask me questions about what does happen to a person, at the moment, the "Soul" or the "Mind" leaves her/his body? Does the "Soul" hang around for a while, or it goes straight to hell or heaven?
A more stimulating and unexpected question – in that context – came from a skeptic currently residing in Madrid, who never believed in anything Anunnaki. He asked me, word for word: "I know what will happen to me when I die. My soul leaves my body, and goes to heaven, because I am a good Catholic. Now, you tell me what happens to an Anunnaki when he dies.
I am particularly interested in what happens to the body and soul of this or that Anunnaki you claim is living here among us? Does he go to heaven?"
The truth is, long time ago, and while I was at the Ulema Ma'had (School), I heard a novice from Burma asking my Ulema teacher, similar questions, perhaps more colorful.
The student asked the honorable Master: "Does your Anunnaki teacher who visits with you on earth die like all of us? And if he

dies on earth, like all of us, does he leave his dead body on earth to be cremated? Or the Anunnaki will come to earth to take his body?"

Quite interesting questions indeed.

I have never heard any spiritual channeler, or a so-called "Psychic Extraterrestrial medium" discussing these subjects, and/or explaining what exactly does happen to the body of an extraterrestrial, and especially an Anunnaki, when she/he dies on earth, despite their fantasmagoric and far-fetched theories visions, jargons and warnings about the Anunnaki!

Did the Ulema address these issues?

Of course they did. Honorable Master Sorenstein said, that in the Ulemite and Ana'kh literature, there are two important words or terms that refer to these situations. These two words are: Kusir and Lalladu."

2. Kusir and Lalladu:

a. Meaning of Kusir: Also Kiaba as it appeared in the "Book of Ramadosh".

De Lafayette said, "Kusir is a term for the physical manifestation of a dead person, before entering another dimension, and/or during the 40 day period following his/her death. The Anunnaki-Ulema said that there are two categories of Kusir:

- **Kusir-Ra:** A physical projection of a dead human being who died from a natural cause. This apparition occurs when the etheric-plasmic body of a deceased person (Any age, any gender) has retained enough particles-energy to manifest its previous physical form. Usually, it appears before relatives and loved ones.

Pets also can re-appear before their owners; however, their physical projection is not always complete.

Quite often some parts of their bodies are missing.

- **Kusir-Ji:** A physical projection of a deceased killed by acts of violence, suicide, and similar tragic means.

The apparition occurs via an ectoplasmic/holographic projection, and/or particles' condensation. But it lasts briefly, for the energy

contained in the apparition or the projection is not strong enough to last for more than 5 seconds.
Usually, entities and/or human shapes that reappear through Kusir-Ji reflect au aura of sadness and confusion. In this state of mind, the deceased is not fully convinced that he/she is in fact dead.

b. Meaning of Lalladu: Lalladu is a term referring to the final moment when an Anunnaki-Ulema, or an Anunnaki-Hybrid relinquishes her/his earthly body, before departing Earth.
Some occultists describe this phenomenon as a disintegration of the molecules of the body, and the "Conduit" in the physical body, at the time of the death of an Anunnaki, temporarily sojourning in a physical dimension like Earth.
According to Ulema Al Saddik, "An Anunnaki-Ulema does not leave a dead physical body behind her/him."

Note: There is an interesting reference to this phenomenon, in the book "Anunnaki Ultimatum", I co-authored with Dr. Ilil Arbel.
Here is an authorized excerpt from the epilogue of the book: Farewell to Victoria.

Note: Victoria is an Anunnaki-Hybrid woman who has lived on Earth for several years. She was known to her friend as Victoria. Her Anunnaki's name is Ambar Anati. In fact, she lived in Lower Manhattan, in New York City, and had two meetings with the US government in Northwest Georgetown, in Washington, D.C. In the epilogue, Ambar Anati explained what exactly happens to an Anunnaki dead body.

Here is the text:
"The most amazing revelations we have heard so far, when the time has come to say goodbye to our dear friend (Ambar Anati) whom we have grown to love.
It was a gray early afternoon, and it looked as if a storm was gathering.
We (Dr. Arbel and Maximillien de Lafayette) were at the office, working on various projects. It was a couple of weeks since last time we talked to Victoria, but generally she called in the early evening, so we did not expect to hear from her quite yet. Suddenly the phone rang, and there she was, to our surprise.

From the first moment, we knew that this telephone call was not one of our usual sessions. Victoria just did not sound the same. As our readers probably know by now, she is usually calm, pleasant, and can say the most amazing, even harrowing things with the most matter-of-fact simplicity to which, by now, we have become quite accustomed. But this time her voice was strained, and she seemed to be in a hurry.

"What is it, Victoria? What is wrong?" we asked.

"My friends, I have come to say goodbye. This is the last time I will be able to talk to you."

"What happened? Are you in need of help? Can we do anything?"

"I am a hunted woman, to tell the truth," said Victoria. "I exploded a contaminated air base, killed many contaminated people. I tried to warn them, one last time, but instead of listening, they decided to lock me up until I died of claustrophobia. It's time for me to leave."

"So why don't you get in touch with Nibiru, and have Sinhar Marduchk come and get you in his space ship?" we asked.

"Because saving me and taking me to Nibiru will not be enough to make me survive," said Victoria.

"Are you wounded?"

"No, that would be nothing. I can heal wounds on my own, like all Anunnaki."

"So is there anything else wrong? Do you need medical attention? We can get a doctor and say nothing about who you are."

"No, I am quite well," said Victoria. "I am not sure how to explain this... well, the point is, the time has come and I must die, right here on earth."

We both jumped to our feet. "Die? Why must you die? Surely with your superior powers you can best any humans who want to harass you?"

"It's not that... You see, after what happened, I cannot stay on earth, and with this body, I cannot live on Nibiru and still achieve the long life I have been promised if I become a full Anunnaki. And to become a full Anunnaki, I must die.

But there is more to this than just the practical aspect. By living here for so long, by associating with the Grays, Hybrids, and contaminated humans, I am contaminated myself.

I have to get rid of all this filth. If Marduchk just takes me to Nibiru, and I change into the new body, I will still carry some of the contamination to Nibiru."

We were confused. If she wishes to live a long life, how can she die? We did not even know what to ask, and waited for her to continue.

"My body will die. But my mind, loaded with the imprint of my DNA, will not die. It will rush to a place we call the Ba'ab. This word in Ana'kh means gate, and I believe it was adopted by various languages on Earth.

The Ba'ab is something like, but not exactly, a white wormhole. Things can pass from one universe to another, or traverse huge distances, through the Ba'ab, in a blink of an eye."

"And what happens to your mind when it passes through the Ba'ab?" we asked.

"Everything has to be fully coordinated," said Victoria, "or else, the mind can be lost in the universe. They will wait for me on Nibiru, with a body-copy they have already prepared years ago.
This body, incidentally, is full Anunnaki, without any human characteristics, as I committed myself to many years ago when I married Marduchk.

My mind, which on Earth you will probably refer to as my soul, must hit the Ba'ab at the absolute right moment, pass through it, and in a split second enter the body-copy. Otherwise, I will be lost.

They may look for me, and perhaps even find me, but the odds are against it; the universe is just too vast. Therefore, I must hit the Ba'ab properly.

It would have been easier if I were transferring from my body into a copy on Nibiru, with Sinhar Inannaschamra to direct me, since she is an expert on such things. But I have no choice, since my Earth body must remain here.

In other words, I simply must die. Unfortunately, I am not experienced with navigating the Ba'abs. But I must take the chance. I must risk it."

By that time we were crying. "So why not stay here, in hiding? At least live out your life before you chance it all?"

Victoria sighed. "I am sixty years old," she said, "and while sixty is not old by any means, I have lived a very intense life for the last thirty years. My body is worn out, and I am very tired. I am willing to take the risk."

"And what about your son?"

"I finally have to realize that I must give him up, let him live his own life, stop worrying about him. He will be fine, he is young, he will do his work for which he was conceived, and later prepared from birth and on.

There are a couple of options for him.

I believe the Anunnaki will destroy the Earth in 2022, and only the uncontaminated will survive. Of course, in this case, he will be saved. If there is a postponement of the destructions, another option exists.

By the time he is relatively old, and his work done, we will come for him, since he is really one hundred percent Anunnaki, and he deserves some reward after a life in service of humanity. Not too many Anunnaki are so inclined..."

"Why is that so?"

"The Anunnaki still love you, deep down, since you are their creations. But they are very strongly disappointed in humanity. The cruelty which humanity expresses is more like the Grays' than the Anunnaki's, who revere all life. You torture, you kill, you abuse the children and the elderly, and you eat animal bodies.

The greed and disloyalty that you express would have been easier to bear, for the Anunnaki, they would have been willing to teach you how to overcome it, but not the viciousness. And yet, they will still help, intervene, at least sometimes, and wait until such time when humanity wakes up and realizes that the atrocities must stop. Then the Anunnaki will return and bring long life, health, and joy. But not before."

"But won't you miss your son?"

"Of course I will, but I have learned that it is essential not to be too strongly tied to anything on Earth. There have been Anunnaki who got attached to things of the flesh, or to personal associations, to such an extent that they have lost their Anunnaki spirit and are still wandering Earth, thousands of years later, unable to reconnect with their true home."

"But Victoria, how will we know that you have reached the Ba'ab and entered your body-copy? We would not be able to bear not knowing. The thought that your beautiful soul might be lost is too much."

"If I succeed, if I am not lost, I will give you a sign. Let's agree on a very clear one. Let's see...I know! Do you have houseplants in the office?"

"Yes, many, on a large and sunny windowsill."

"Then when all is accomplished, every single one of your houseplants will burst into bloom, even those that normally have no flowers. And the lights will flicker three times, off and on." She laughed, and we laughed with her, with tears in our eyes.

"How will you die, Victoria? You won't be in pain, will you?"

"Oh, no. I was told to go to a place that has water, trees, and flowers. I will sit under a tree, close my eyes, and my mind will separate from my body, quite peacefully. They taught me how to do it and promised me that it will be entirely painless."

"It is rainy and dark here. Are you somewhere warm and sunny? Will you get wet and uncomfortable?"

"No, I am far away from you. It's sunny and pleasant here. The tree I am going to sit under is a big, beautiful willow."

"Will you sleep? Will you feel anything?"

"Oh, no, I have to be fully aware of the circumstances to be able to do the job. I will be completely alert, and in an instant, I will use my Conduit to enter the Ba'ab, if all goes well."

"Will your body be found by anyone?"

"I have no idea, it really does not matter in any way, it's just a body; perhaps it will disintegrate, who knows."

"May we ask where it is going to happen? Perhaps we could go there afterwards, just to feel that we have been with you?"

"You are so kind, my friends, but no, I can't tell you, I am not permitted. You see, in the very distance past, humans thought that the Anunnaki were gods. You know some of their names – Inanna, Enlil, Ninlil, El... of course they were not gods, they were Anunnakis, and as a matter of fact, they are alive and well on Nibiru, engaged in their new missions.

One name I daresay you already recognize from my story, but we will not dwell on it, or she may be angry with me. At any rate, if my place of death is discovered, how are we to be sure that it won't some day become a place of worship, when humanity is just a little more attuned to the Anunnaki again?

We can't risk that. But please don't be upset with me about it. After all, I won't be there. I will be flying to my destiny in Nibiru through the Ba'ab."

"It's so hard to part from you, Victoria. Will you ever be in touch again?"

"Who knows? If I survive, I might see you in 2022."

"Are you sure we will be alive then?"

"Oh, yes. I have already taken care to extend your lives. This will happen to all the surviving humans when the Anunnaki come back. You will experience a much, much longer lifespan."

"How wonderful and kind of you. And it is so strange to think about a very long lifespan..."

"The universe is so full of strange things, strange phenomena," said Victoria. "I will always love you and think kindly of you, no matter what happens."

"But you will be a full Anunnaki. Won't you lose your human interests?"

"I have always been almost a full Anunnaki, to tell the truth. My DNA was ninety percent Anunnaki. From the time I enter my new body, I will be a hundred percent Anunnaki. They will probably start calling me by my Anunnaki name, Sinhar Ambar-Anati.

I hope Marduchk doesn't and goes on calling me Victoria... it will feel so strange to have him call me by a new name. Incidentally, the only reason I was human in my views is because I was raised by humans.

But think about it, I never cared about so many things humans care about, such as money, or sex, or possessions. That I am hoping, with all my heart, that humanity will learn to change its ways and that we should all meet again. You know by now that death really does not exist, even if you can't fully grasp it. Someday you shall."

"When will your death happen, Victoria?"

"In a few minutes, I expect. I am now sitting under the willow, talking on my cell phone, and I am still acting like a normal human being; a woman talking on a cellular phone! Incidentally, I have a gift for you, which I have already mailed you a couple of days ago and you should receive shortly. It is something you will like very much, and it was sent with the blessings and approval of my husband. A surprise!"

"Goodbye, Victoria," we said, crying. "Good bye and a safe, good trip. We are watching with you." But she was no longer on the phone.

We sat in silence.

Will she make it to the gate?

Would the Ba'ab open for her?

Would our dear friend make it to her new body and be warmly welcomed by her family, or would she forever wander the universe, alone, homeless?

We waited for the sign, breathlessly. We had no idea how long it would take. Suddenly the doorbell rang, and the mailman came with a package. We knew what it was. It had to be Victoria's last gift. What could it be?

We opened the package carefully, and inside were two notebooks and a letter. "Dear friends," said the letter. "This is the facsimile of the professional diary of my husband, containing much about his work over many years.

It should be very useful for you in your future work, and you are allowed to reveal anything you wish from it to humanity, with Marduchk's fond wishes that it may help humanity overcome its flaws and grow in the right direction.

The small book is a dictionary. We know that Ana'kh is a difficult language, and the dictionary may help. Enjoy both! With love, Victoria."

We looked at the books with reverence, trying to decipher the words. The large notebook had a title, which we understood to be "Sinhar Marduchk's Diary."

The small book was titled something like "Lexicon of the Ana'kh Language." Understanding the books should take some time, it was obvious, but what a treasure. Naturally, thought, we could not concentrate. It was already about fifteen minutes after our conversation with Victoria. Surely, by now she would either have succeeded – or she has failed...

The tension was too much to bear, and yet there was nothing we could do but wait. She said, a few minutes... it was much later than that. We were losing our hope. It became dark in the office, the clouds were driven by the wind and became a heavy layer.

We turned on the light and just sat there, waiting...tears in our eyes.

Suddenly, the light flickered. We looked up, hoping against hope. Could it just be the brewing storm?

It flickered again.

The thunder rolled, and the rain started falling down in sheets. And then it flickered for the third time.

There was no question, it had to be her sign – and at this instant, without warning, the room filled with intense floral

scent. We ran to the window sill. Every single plant was covered with immense flowers – yellow, white, rose, red – flowers that were never seen on Earth, flowers that had to come straight from paradise – or from Nibiru, or from Victoria's heart.
Victoria has made it home."

*** *** ***

75. Reading Past, Present, and Future Events From the Life of one Single Person
"La-abrida"
"Bzi'ra-irdu"
⌘ ⌘ ⌘

1. Definition and introduction
2. Synopsis of mode of operation
3. The beginning of everything; multiples existences and "God's Particle"
4. La-abrida "Bzi'ra-irdu"; is it a tool to go back in time or jump into the future?
5. Can I use La-abrida "Bzi'ra-irdu" to ameliorate my life, and change my destiny?
6. Revisiting your childhood in another dimension, in another time
7. The invisible and thin quantum line dividing two space-time dimensions
8. Q&A

75. Reading Past, Present, and Future Events From the Life of one Single Person
"La-abrida"
"Bzi'ra-irdu"
⌘⌘⌘

1. Definition and introduction
2. Synopsis of mode of operation
3. The beginning of everything; multiples existences and "God's Particle"
4. La-abrida "Bzi'ra-irdu"; is it a tool to go back in time or jump into the future?
5. Can I use La-abrida"Bzi'ra-irdu" to ameliorate my life, and change my destiny?
6. Revisiting your childhood in another dimension, in another time
7. The invisible and thin quantum line dividing two space-time dimensions
8. Q&A

---

1. Definition and introduction:
As stated verbatim by Ulema Maximillien de Lafayette:
A rectangular glass table, that resonates, when metallic cards are placed on its surface.

- The word "glass" is hereby used for lack of proper terminology. The material is transparent like glass, but the substance is very different, and cannot be described, using our Earth's vocabularies.
- The "metallic cards" represent thin and encoded boards. The word "metallic" is hereby used, for lack of proper terminology.

- Each card contains sequences of numbers and dots, perforated on one side of each card.
- Misinformed researchers nicknamed the cards "Galactic Tarot". It is incorrect.
- The cards project and interpret sequences and passages from an individual's life in one particular dimension; one space-time sphere at the time.
- Duplicate, and/or multiple projections of different lives in different dimensions are also possible.
- However, the projection of any of a person's multiple lives existing in separate universes has no bearing or any effect on the current existence in the third dimension.
- Alteration of past events in a different dimension does not categorically alter current events in the third dimension.
- However, the results and direct consequences of such alteration could and would cange the course of life, and events to occur in the present and the near future of an individual, if the person's "Conduit" (Brain cell Conduit) is activated.
- On Earth, a person could be an illustrious writer, while in a second or a parallel dimension; the very same person is totally illiterate. People live different lives in different dimensions.
- On Earth, a person for instance is a distinguished judge, while in another dimension; the very same person is an outlaw.
- Removing, altering and/or erasing a crime committed by a person in another dimension does not categorically "clean", and/or delete the "Galactic Record" of that person on the "Conscience-Cosmic-Net". That person is still held liable for his/her action, and will be punished for his/her crime.
- For instance, on Earth (Third dimension), you are 40 year old, while in the same time, you could be 60 year old, or not even born, in another dimension (Universe).
- In some dimensions, Alexander the Great is still on his way to ancient Persia, and Jesus is not yet crucified.
- The sequences constitute the code.
- The code is the key to a wide variety of information and data about individuals.

- In other words, each card could be interpreted as a microchip.
- The microchip stores every single event (Past, present and future) in the life of a person, including, duplications of similar or different occurrences on other planes.
- "Other planes" mean a separate form of existence in a parallel dimension.
- "Resonate" means responding to the placement of the card upon the surface of the glass table.
- "Responding" means, reading and/or deciphering the code (Key to information) of the data and information stored in each card.

*** *** ***

2. Synopsis of mode of operation:
Ulema de Lafayette said:
- La abrida "Bzi'ra-irdu", functions like "Miraya", "Minzar", and "Mnaizar".
- However, the use of the La-abrida is limited to reading past, present, and future events in the life of one single person.
- When a card is placed on the top of the glass table, the card changes properties, shape and form.
- The "metallic" structural substance of the card becomes translucent, and merges with the glass surface.
- To the naked eye, it appears as if the card was totally absorbed by the glass surface. However, the size of the card remains intact.
- The shape of the card becomes circular, but retains its original size, meaning, each card occupies the same space, before the shape was changed.
- Thus, the form of the card becomes either circular or conical.
- Almost instantly, conic pages open up on the glass surface of the table. Usually, three to four pages, aligned horizontally.
- Each page has a distinct color, ranging from light green to almost transparent blue.

- Words, geometric symbols, dots, and numbers appear on each page.
- They are the data and information pertaining to the "existence" of one person in multiple spheres (Separate existences in multiple life-form universes.)
- This means, that individuals (Humans and animals alike) do live separately and independently as 4 distinct living persons in 4 distinct dimensions, or more.
- Contemporary quantum physics theorists totally accept this reality. Many books and articles discussed this incomprehensible phenomenon.
- The multiple and separate existences (In our case, 4) are called in quantum physics membranes, or simply branes.
- Each membrane represents a separate world, called dimension in contemporary quantum physics. In other words, that dimension refers to "another universe".
- So far, quantum physics theorists have accepted the notion that, there are 11 dimensions in our universe.
- On the glass surface of the La abrida "Bzi'ra-irdu", the adept will be able to see (In miniature) four different dimensions.
- Each one of them, containing a duplicate (Identical or totally different) of himself or herself, his or her total life, habitat, physical appearance, preoccupations, and environment.
- In other words, the adept is watching simultaneously his/her other four existences/lives in four separate universes. And this concept has become a major part of the modern study and research of cosmology, and quantum physics, usually discussed under various theories, such as the "Multiverse", the "M Theory", the "String Theory", the "Membranes Theory," so on.

3. The beginning of everything:
Multiples existences and "God's Particle".

Ulema Haroon Bakri bin Rached Al Ansari, and Ulema Mordechai ben Zvi provided the following explanation.
Herewith reproduced verbatim, word for word, and unedited. Taken from their Kira'at (Readings), Kiramat Ketab (Book of the good deeds), Hadith (Speech; dialogue) and Rou'ya (Visions; insight):

- Time is not linear. Thus, the landscape of so called time and space is not the same in other worlds.
- In multiple universes, the past, the present, and the future are all contained in one particle.
- This particle is the "Cell of Everything".
- This means, everything that has existed before, and shall exist afterward. It is the origin of the creation.
- The particle is the beginning of everything that is everlasting. Quantum physics theorists call this cell or particle the "God's Particle".
- In this cell, you will find all the "Bubbles" (Term used by modern cosmologists) that collided together to create all the universes, galaxies, and planets in the cosmos.
- Who created the God's Particle?
- Who created the universe?
- Who created time?
- Who crerated "God"?
- Is there one single Creator who created everything in the universe, including humans and non-humans?
- The God's particle was at the beginning of everything. And everything was not in existence. Thus, before the particle, time did not exist, space did not exist, the past did not exist, the future did not exist, humans did not exist, and religions did not exist; in brief nothing existed.
- The Universe was not created by one single creator. The universe was not created by a "Big Bang."
- The universe emerged from itself, from within.
- And when, the nothingness of existence of all forms and substances suddenly collided with itself, the whole universe exploded into billions and billions of stars, galaxies, planets, and layers of dimensions.
- In some universes, the coagulation of time with the landscape of space created time.
- When time was created by the collision of universes (Bubbles), galaxies and universes took shape and place in the cosmos.
- On some planets, and in some galaxies, photosynthesis, metabolism, followed by micro-biological evolution created multiple life-forms everywhere.

- Some of these life-forms produced all kinds and shapes of organic and botanic substances, stones, mountains, gases, waters, atmospheres. In some dimensions, different intelligent life forms were created.
- We call this intelligent life-form "Kir-Ra-Ibra", meaning the faculty of reasoning and creating.
- The primordial intelligent life-form belonged to very advanced galactic races inhabiting billions of stars and planets.
- Billions of years later, the human race was genetically created by some of these very advanced intelligent life-forms, such as the Anunnaki, Igigi, and Lyrans.
- When pre-humans, proto-humans, and quasi-human began to populate the Earth, time did not exist at that point in history.
- Later, much later, when the Lyrans, Igigi, and the Anunnaki commenced to experiment with the archaic human species (They were 47 different categories), they installed in the brain of the human beings, some form of intelligence.
- Some early humans were fortunate to receive the "Conduit", the invisible cell in the brain that produces all sorts of human activities and thoughts.
- When the early human beings began to reason, the notion of time was conceived.
- Thus, "Time" became the invention of humans.
- Time exists on Earth, not on other dimensions.

4. La-abrida "Bzi'ra-irdu":
Is it a tool to go back in time or jump into the future?
Is it physical or ethereal?

Ulema Maximillien de Lafayette explained:
- No. Because, if you want to go back in time, and/or visit the future, you have to depart from this dimension (Earth), where you currently live.
- Once, you are outside the perimeter of the third dimension (Earth), time bends on itself.
- Space bends on itself. And you are caught in the middle.

- However, you can escape this dilemma, and realign yourself, following the cadence/rhythm of all dimensions beyond the third one.
- How, will you accomplish this? We will elaborate on this, when we study the "Parallel Synchronization."
- Since time does not exist, the enlightened ones (Many of you are enlightened) will be able to watch themselves living separately in different worlds.
- This is what La abrida "Bzi'ra-irdu" does. It allows you to "see" not to revisit the past or jump into the future, unless your "Conduit" is fully activated.
- Once you are outside the physical realm (Earth), you immediately connect with the beginning of everything in the universe.
- You become part of "God's Particle."
- However, and as we have explained before, revisiting the so-called past is possible if you use the Gomatirach Minzari.
- But bear in mind, you are not visiting, but transposing yourself, unless your "Conduit" is fully activated.

5. Can I use the "La-abrida" to ameliorate my life, and change my destiny?

"Yes," said Ulema Kanazawa.

He added, verbatim: "However, you cannot alter the laws of cause and effect; something similar to what you call Karma, but in reality, it is quite different from Karma, because there is no place for reincarnation in the world of the Anunnaki.

There are the Anunnaki's norms that remain universal wherever you go, although they are norms per se, but not necessary cosmic laws.

- On Earth, you are accountable for all your actions.
- The same applies in all the dimensions, realms, and spheres of time, and space.
- However, in a different form of existence, or dimension, the nature and understanding of certain moral and ethical laws might change considerably.
- Such change has a paramount effect on the level of enlightenment and happiness you wish to reach.

- On Earth, we have what we call the human law, the natural law, and dogma establishing acceptable behavior in societies and communities.
- These laws quite often change in virtue of our understanding of what is right, and what is wrong. They also change, as time changes, as our form of government changes, as a majority's power and influence change, regionally and nationally.
- Nothing is truthfully permanent on Earth.
- In the galactic perimeter of advanced and "spiritual" communities, values do not change. They are permanent and universal, and they govern the general conduct of life-forms and intelligent entities, in the entire universe.
- If you enter a particular dimension, far away from Earth, or too close to Earth, you might encounter social rules that are in sharp contrast with laws on Earth.
- This could confuse your mind, and prevent you from understanding and/or recognizing what is right, and what is wrong.
- If this should happen to you, you will not be able to ameliorate your life, and change your destiny, when you return to Earth, and/or to the present.
- Something else you should take into consideration.
- What kind of destiny, success, happiness, prosperity and advancement are you talking about?
- Are they those your are aiming at, upon returning to Earth, or those you are seeking after death? Or, possibly those that exist in a dimension close to Earth?
- The Anunnaki-Ulema can simultaneously live in two or three different dimensions, and coordinate their actions via the "Conduit".
- We call this, the "Universal Conduit".
- Humans have not yet reached a level of morality and "spirituality" that allows them to live and relive in separate dimensions at the same time.
- Although, some humans might be invited to visit another dimension and acquire a great deal of knowledge, wisdom, and even supernatural powers, upon their return to Earth, they will instantly forget whatever they have learned, heard and seen, unless they are spiritually developed, and guided by the enlightened ones.

- Thus, in order to ameliorate you destiny, prosper in your endeavors, and preserve a good health, you must be able to differentiate between what is right and what is wrong, at a galactic level.
- You must become acquainted with the universal truth; the galactic harmony of things.
- Truth in the "outer cosmos" is quite different from the truth you find on Earth.
- Only your activated "Conduit" will allow you to do so.
- There also certain measures and requirements you must consider and comply with, before you leave Earth and enter another dimension, and/or time-space sphere.
- For instance, selecting the correct time to revisit the past, and/or another dimension is paramount.
- What "Ba'ab" (Door or entrance to the other world) shall you enter?
- How shall you adapt, correct or adjust your vision in a new dimension?
- How would you differentiate between an astral travel, imagination, fantasy of your mind, and reality?
- Even in highly developed dimensions, and in many different time/space spheres, you will encounter fantasy, tricks of the mind, hallucinations, and fake apparitions.
- Many of the other dimensions (Plans) and time-space spheres are similar to Earth, even though the structural composition and their properties are enormously different.
- All these encounters, images and feelings will prevent your mind from understanding what you are seeing. You will be totally confused.
- For example, and let's assume for now, that you have managed to go back in time, and visit with people and societies from the 18th century.
- First, how would you know, that the people you will see there are indeed from the 18th century, and not people just like you, visiting the past for the first time?
- Second, how would you guide yourself, direct yourself, and reach your destination, without getting lost?

- Bear in mind, that in a different dimension, you will not have enough time to find your way around, if you don't have the map of the afterlife, and parallel dimensions.
- Third, you will not be able to last long over there, because your mind and your body will run out of energy.
- Besides, do you know how to charge and/or recharge yourself?
- You will be facing incomprehensible situations similar to ectoplasmic apparitions.
- Quite often, these ectoplasmic apparitions/projections (Complete or partial) dissipate because the entity has rapidly consumed its "apparition and manifestation energy."
- Once you have completed your orientation program, and the master has activated your "Conduit", your trip to the past or to another dimension will be successful and very beneficial.

*** *** ***

6. Revisiting your childhood in another dimension, in another time:

Master Kanazawa explained this in one of his Kira'at (Readings/Lectures).

Here is what he said to his students, verbatim, word for word, and unedited:

- Copy of your childhood is still real and vivid in another dimension.
- This image is still there. It is your image when you were a child.
- It is physical and real.
- Even the toys and candies you loved are still there, and they are real too.
- You can even touch those toys and play with them if you want.
- You can grab your favorite candies from the jar and eat one.
- Everything you see and taste is real.
- You are not hallucinating, and your mind is not playing tricks on you.

- How can you be so sure?
- It is simple, and very convincing, because upon meeting people you knew while you were child, you will be able to tell them how did they live and what they did when they were young like you, in the same town, around the same corner, and even describe to them the kind of games you played with them in the streets, in the school yard, and on the streets sidewalks.
- You will be able to tell them what they did on that particular Sunday day, after the church service.
- But you will see it and enjoy it only once, because you might not be able to return once again to that dimension.
- Sometime, it is so easy to enter the extra-dimension of your youth, without training.
- Sometime, it happens, just like that, because you have escaped the gravity of time on Earth.
- It is a sudden opening into your past.
- A past you have lived here on Earth, and was duplicated somewhere else.
- Now, you are revising that "somewhere else", and nobody is going to recognize it, except you.
- You will recognize all the people you will be seeing and meeting in that "somewhere elsewhere" dimension. But, they will not recognize you.
- Even though, you give them very particular and personal details about their lives, their habits, the place where they grew up, the name of that school teacher they like, of that math teacher they hated.
- Still, they will not believe that you are the one you claim or pretend to be; a friend from their youth, a real friend from your past, or their past; a past you really shared with them.
- But remember, there is always one person who will believe you. And he is always around you.
- Perhaps, it is the other copy of yourself, or your guardian angel?
- You will have the chance to meet that "other copy of yourself" in some other time, and somewhere else...in another dimension.

- The name of the store you are revisiting now in that dimension has not changed. Perhaps, only the name of the proprietor did. Because the former owner was already too old, and he passed away some twenty years ago.
- You used to come to that store, sit on the stool, and talk to Mr. Ted, the old owner of the store.
- "Mr. Ted passed away long time ago," will tell you the man standing behind the counter in the store.
- But the truth is, Mr. Ted is somewhere else now, exactly as you are somewhere else, in other dimension.
- Something very strange will happen to you in that dimension. You could see yourself as a child riding that beautiful old carousel. Or perhaps chasing an old car.
- Those images are real. Because you will recognize them in their most intimate details.
- Some other people will agree with you when you describe to them the carousel you loved, the kind of cars people drove in that small town, and the name of those teachers you have mentioned.
- Yet, they will never believe you when you tell them, that you grew up here, how you used to chase that old Impala Chevrolet of Mr. Evans, and those treasured comics books you bought from Mrs. Adams, who used to own the little bookstore around the corner.
- It is up to you to believe what you are seeing or to totally reject it.
- But if you reject it, you will never be able to revisit your youth, and other worlds, small towns, and cities you lived in before.
- You begin to ask yourself, how did you get there? How did you get here in the other dimension?
- You start to question your sanity.
- But you know deep down, you are not dreaming, and you are not hallucinating, because the people you see are real, and they walk and they talk like real people.
- Only their hairdo has changed, the fashion of their clothes is old, old enough to send you back in time. The cars you see are old too, they are 1930's model. And the calligraphy style of the names of the shops on windows and doors is old too.

- So what are you going to do in that strange place?
- You put your hands in your pockets, and you will find dimes and nickels. Because that was all what you needed to buy an ice cream or a candy.
- Then you begin to wonder why people are not believing you.
- You have told them true stories about people they knew, stories about you and your parents, and about everything you saw and you did when you were a child in that town.
- It is very likely, you will meet your parents before they were married.
- You will recognize your mother, or at least your mother to be.
- You call her by her name, her maiden name and her married name. You will scare her, and she will think you are insane.
- How would you or could you convince her you are her child?
- How would you convince her that she was the mother who fed you, who clothed you and took you to the movie house "Rex" with your sisters, and kept on telling you to keep quiet while watching the movie, because you talked too much.
- You tell her all this, yet, she will not believe you.
- But just before you leave her, she feels something she can't explain.
- These encounters and deja vu experiences happened to many people before.
- If you anchor them in your mind, in your "Conduit", you will be able to return and visit with them once again, but it will happen in a different dimension.
- A dimension, where your mother is no longer your mother, but possibly your date, or just another woman?
- Confusing? You bet.
- But this is what constitutes the fabric of time and space in other dimensions. A time and a space that cease to exist in that dimension.
- A dimension not very far from where you currently live.

7. The invisible quantum line dividing two space-time dimensions:

- The invisible thin quantum line dividing two times capsules, both located on the same plane, is usually the outer limit of two dimensions.
- These two time-space dimensions are usually found in isolated areas, such as distant valleys, fields, and spots on Earth, rarely visited by the public.
- The two time-capsules represent two different time intervals and all past events that occurred separately in each one of them.
- Even sounds from past eras can be heard separately, coming from each one of them.
- You can't see the diving line. It is not visible to the naked eye.
- If you cross that line, you leave the time you are living in, and you enter a different time-space.
- This is the time and space where you can change the past, but rarely does it happen, unless in previous times, you were part of the past, and/or have witnessed these events from the past.
- For instance, you are in 1974, on one time-capsule section of the land (Field, desert, spot). You cross the line separating 1974 and another year, perhaps hundreds of years.
- You cross the line and you enter another time without knowing it.
- Once in, you become part of the past, and a real person from the past. You are as real as all the physical things you see before your eyes.
- The events or scenes you will see are usually memorable, meaningful, historical, or important events known to you. You are very familiar with what you are currently seeing.
- They appear from nowhere, and since you have become part of the past, these events become factual.
- Part of your mind will tell you that you know a lot about these events, because you have read about these events, but you can't remember where and when.

- Another part of your mind convinces you that you are seeing the true events as they have happened, or you are seeing the events for the first time.
- This is a moment of confusion for you. But eventually you will sort it out.
- Is it a mirage? A hallucination? A fantasy? Or the real thing? Well, if you have stepped in the true time-capsule sphere, then, what you are seeing is real, and what you are feeling is not psychosomatic but truly physical.
- Many people have reported that some of their friends have vanished walking this dividing line. And the missing persons were never found, because they have entered another dimension, never to return again.
- In the Anunnaki's "Donia" (Spheres; world), there is no hallucination, coincidence, fantasy, or psychosomatic effects. Everything is tested and real.
- If for some reasons, the "Ba'ab" (Door; stargate) of time-space opens up before you, and you were instantly transported or absorbed into its dimension, you instantly become an inseparable part of that dimension.
- You will relive the events and time of that dimension.
- If at the time, when you were transported, a battle was going on, you become one of those men who are fighting in this battle. Each scene that appears before your eyes will blend you in its fabric and time-reality, and you will not be able to escape its boundaries.
- How real are these events? They are real 100%.
- Are you really seeing a real battle? Affirmative.
- What if for some reasons you took part in this battle, is there a possibility that you could get killed? Really killed?
- Absolutely. Because in that dimension, you are not a spectator, or a visitor, but a real person transposed and transported to a real battle field.
- It is hard, even impossible for humans to understand this mystery. But it is happening for real in another dimension.
- Yes, you could die in that dimension, but you are still alive in another one, because all of us live simultaneously in different dimensions.

- Probably now you are asking whether the person who died in that battle is in fact the same person who is still alive in 1978 or 1979 or even in the future.
- And my answer is yes. You are all these persons in all these capsule-time spheres.
- You are the same person, but the properties of your body are different, as dictated by each dimension respectively.
- Another time-scene might open before you, for example, an old city market or bazaar. The shoppers, the stores, the goods, and everything you see is real.
- You look at yourself and you realize that you are wearing clothes of the era. Yet, part of your mind that has retained space-time memory will tell you that you are living real events and real time, but you are just visiting another time and space in history.
- Then, if this is the scenario, can you go back to where you came from? Yes, you can.
- One way to do it is by using the Gomatirach-minzari, and similar techniques. (Note: See Gomatirach-minzari, on page 83 in the book "Ramadosh Book; 13 Anunnaki-Ulema Mind Power Techniques to Live Longer, Happier, Healthier, Wealthier.)

8: Q&A:
At the end of Master Kanazawa' Kira'at (Reading/Lecture), a young student asked the Master: "Master, it is possible to bring with me, something from that dimension I have visited, so when I tell my friends about it they would believe me?"
"Of course you can," replied the Master. "And this is how many ancient artifacts were brought back to the present. Some ended in the basements of museums, others dissipated in the doubtful minds of humans who could live only once."
Another young student asked Honorable Master Kanazawa: "Master, you told us that sometimes, we enter a different dimension without knowing how to do it. You said, it happens just like that. Why? And if this happens just like that, then our "Conduit" does not need to be activated to visit other worlds?"

The perplexed student paused for a short moment, and asked again: "Master, when we get there, do we go to different levels in the same dimension, or is it one single dimension we see all the time? And how many different worlds can we visit in a single trip to the past or to other dimensions?"

The Honorable Master replied (As is, verbatim, word for word, and unedited):
- Everything depends on how your brain is wired.
- If your "Conduit" has been activated, then, you will know and understand what is happening to you, and all the things you will see in the other world(s) will be assimilated gradually by your brain.
- To understand what it is actually happening there, and how you got there, you have to visualize your mind as a tall building with many floors.
- Inside the building, there is an elevator that goes all the way to the highest floor.
- There is only one single elevator for all the people who enter the building.
- Each floor represents one layer of that dimension (The other world).
- This does not mean that the dimension you have entered has sub-divisions or additional dimensions. Simply put, the dimension is divided into multiple spheres, called layers.
- Each sphere gathers different kinds of people, eras, knowledge, events, memories, sensations, cars, shops, streets, so on.
- One floor could be the past universe and past time of the 18th century. Another floor could be the 12th century. And another floor could be the future.
- But for now, do not worry about all these centuries and the future.
- Instead, let's go back to the place on Earth, from which you entered another dimension.
- There are two kinds of entrances to another world.
- The first one occurs through the activation of your "Conduit". And you know already how this happens.
- The second kind of entrance to another world is the accidental one, which is the current situation you are in.

- Usually, the coincidental or accidental entrance to another world occurs from spots and areas on Earth, that are not heavily visited or frequented.
- So, let's assume that you are in a distant field, a valley, a prairie, whatever. And you are just walking in that field.
- For reasons, your mind cannot understand yet, time-space pockets open up before you.
- Some scientists call these pockets vorteces.
- In our Ana'kh language, we call them "Ba'abs" (Doors, entrances, time tunnels, etc.)
- When the "Ba'ab" accidentally opens up, a huge but narrow tunnel appears before you.
- This tunnel takes the form of a spiral-wind; a sort of an atmospheric turbulence.
- You will see it.
- You will feel its electro-magnetic field, and before you know it, you are sucked up by its current.
- Once inside the tunnel, your will start to feel as if your body is shrinking. Sometime, just the opposite.
- You will feel as if your body is stretching out intensely.
- Everything depends on the intensity of the tunnel's vacuum power.
- In all cases, you will be transported immediately, to another dimension that resembles the building I told you about before.
- The vacuum power, the tunnel's magnetic field, and the opening of the "Ba'ab", all these phenomena are caused by atmospheric anomalies conditioned and created by the collision of time-space plates.
- For now, consider these time-space plates as the tectonic plates of the Earth, that have caused the Earth to shift so many times throughout the centuries, and to change the superficies, shapes, and locations of continents, oceans, mountains, so on.
- The time-space plates, although invisible to the naked eye, exist at the entrance and borders of all dimensions existing in the universe.
- You can consider them as the landmark(s) of multiple universes.

- When the plates collide, or bump into each other, a time/space-vacuum tunnel opens up immediately.
- In this very particular time/space-vacuum tunnel, all things, physical and non-physical lose their original and primordial properties.
- This means, that your body entering this vacuum is no longer the same body you had on Earth.
- The molecules change.
- Your Nahpsiya (DNA in modern scientific language) is altered.
- The weight and size of your body change instantly.
- In brief, what you retain in you, is only a spatial memory, a sort of a small recollection of things and events that happened to you on Earth.
- Now, you are inside the tunnel.
- Your body zooms inside the tunnel at the speed of light.
- This incomprehensible speed allows you to travel to the edge of the universe.
- And this travel includes all the dimensions and other worlds that have existed and/or shall exist in the future.
- You might land in a world that has existed in the past.
- Once you land there, you will not be able to understand everything you see. But you will realize very clearly, that you are now in a different and a real world.
- Now, we go back to the tall building I told you about before.
- It is very important to remember that building, because we are going to use it as a representation of the other world you are facing now.
- Very good. Now you are right in front of the tall building.
- If you stay in the street, outside the building, you will see only one dimension.
- This dimension could be Egypt in the 3rd century B.C., or Paris in the 18th century. It does not matter.
- Now, you decide to enter the building. You go straight to the elevator and you push the second floor button.
- Very good. The door of the elevator opens up, you step out, and you enter the second floor.
- Although this second floor is still in the same building, the time-space has changed.

- This means, that you are entering another era, another century of Egypt or Paris.
- The place (Country, in this case) does not change.
- You are still in Egypt or in Paris, depending where you have landed first. Egypt is still Egypt. And Paris is still Paris. But the time (Century, in this case) has changed.
- You will get used to it, when you progress in your study.
- Let's assume that you have decided now to take the elevator to the 10th floor.
- What are you going to see on the 10th floor?
- Certainly, neither Egypt or Paris, or anything else you saw on other floors. It is going to be another country.
- What is happening here is this: You are not entering a dimension that represents other worlds from outer space, or beyond the solar system, or beyond the metaphysical world.
- You are still on Earth, but in different time-space intervals, eras, centuries, and possibly locations that no longer exist.
- This is exactly what the building represents.
- And this is exactly what we call going back in time.

*** *** ***

76. Spathe of the Male Date-Palm "Lagishimmar" "Lagi-zulum"
⌘⌘⌘

Also called the deity's hand-bucket.

1. Definition and introduction
2. Symbolism
3. Esoteric and magical use

If you look carefully at the sculptures of the gods and kings of Sumer, Babylon, Mesopotamia, Assyria, Chaldea, so on, you will notice that they always carry something in their hands; a sort of a handbag, a purse, perhaps a bucket? Did you ever wonder why? First, what is "this thing?"
Second, why "this thing" was so important to them? In their Ana'kh/Ulemite language, the Anunnaki-Ulema call "this thing" Lagishimmar "Lagi-zulum".

1. Definition and introduction:
Lagishimmar "Lagi-zulum" means and represents the "Spathe of the Male Date-Palm." A symbol for:
- **a**-A fertile agriculture;
- **b**- Lands and civilization prosperity;
- **c**- Cure for many diseases and illnesses.

From Lagishimmar "Lagi-zulum", derived:
The Old Babylonian/Mesopotamian, Chaldean and Sumerian words:
- **a**- Zulum, which means date;
- **b**- Gishimmar, which means a date palm.

A winged God or Genius holding the "Spathe of the Male Date-Palm."

2. Symbolism:

Lagishimmar "Lagi-zulum" (Spathe of the Male Date-Palm) appeared on many ancient Sumerian, Akkadian, Mesopotamian and Babylonian sculptures, obelisks, inscriptions, texts, clay tablets, and cylinders, such as:

- **1**-The "Eagle-Headed Deity" 883-59 B.C.;

A traditional Mesopotamian, Neo-Assyrian eagle-headed, representing a winged divinity, standing before the Babylonian Tree of Life.
Originally, it was an ornamental carving from a wall in the royal palace of king Nimrud, which was built by the legendary Assurnasirpal II, King of Assyria.

The eagle-headed deity is holding a spathe of date (Palm) tree in one hand, and a bucket in the other. In many instances, both the "bucket" and the Spathe" represent the same thing, such as agriculture development, fertility of the lands of Mesopotamia, and a royal authority.
In other words, it depicts the political power and prosperity of Mesopotamia (Assyria, Chaldea).

- **2**-The "Cylinder Seal with the Winged Su Disk" (White Calcite Cylinder Seal 3200-3000 B.C. Mesopotamia.)

- **3**-The Khorsabad Deity holding a flowing vase", Iraq; Khorsabad, Nabu Temple; Neo-Assyrian Period; Reign of Sargon II, 721-705 B.C. Gypsum. Excavated by the Oriental Institute, in 1932-33.

- **4**- The Legend of Oannes.

- **5**- The "Winged figure from the palace of Sargon of Akkad," in Assyria.

According to G. Maspero, he appears to be holding something which he has just plucked from a sacred plant or tree and has sometimes been described as a fir cone, a sponge, the "Spathe of the Male Date-Palm".

- **6**- Additional illustrations of the bucket or the vessel appeared on inscriptions, cylinders, and statues of

Tiglath Pileser, Sargon, Markuk, Sennacherib, Nimrud, Sardanapalus, Nebuchadnezzar, Asshur (Assur), Shalmaneser, Neriglissar, Nabonidus, Assurbanipal, ShamaspPhul, and Esar Haddon, so on.

Originally and essentially, it represented the "Tree of Life", and became a symbol of:
- **a**-Royal authority,
- **b**-The visible wealth of a nation,
- **c**-Settlement and development of societies,
- **d**-Power of a kingdom,
- **e**-A national pride,
- **f**-And above all, the "Tree of Life".

The "Tree of Life" is the "physical chart, the DNA sequences, and the direct link between humans and their creators, the Anunnaki and the Igigi," said Ulema Al Baydani Tamer bin abi Sufian, and Ulema Saber bin Thabet Al Ghazali.

According to very ancient Near Eastern oral traditions, generated by the Gnostics, and the bishops of early Eastern Christianity in Anatolia, Antioch (Intaquieh), Konia, Adana, Aleppo, Maalula, Kaamishli, Izmir, and Sa'ad-Neyah, the "Solomon's Juice", called in Arabic and proto-Aramaic "Suleiman Shiraab", was the Elixir of Life, wrongly nicknamed ORME by contemporary authors.

*** *** ***

3. Esoteric and magical use by the Anunnaki-Ulema:
The early Anunnaki Ulema used the "Deity's Hand- Bucket", as their secret logo. It appeared in the archaic inscriptions and texts of the "Brotherhood of Melkart", the "Circle of the Fish", the "Serpent Society", in Ugarit, Amrit, Tyre, and Sidon, on the lost cylinder-ring of King Solomon, and particularly in the diagrams of the "Book of Ramadosh."
Symbolically, the "Bucket" represented the water of life; the source of life; the source of all knowledge.

Centuries later, the Anunnaki-Ulema's "Bucket" was introduced in the ancient literature of Babylon, Mesopotamia, Assyria,

Chaldea, Sumer and the lands of the Hittites in Anatolia, and frequently used by the gods and kings of the ancient world of the Near East and the Middle East.

Almost, every Babylonian King had his own "Bucket". And frequently, the Mesopotamian/Babylonian gods, the ancient deities of the region, the monarchs of the ancient Middle/Near East were depicted on cylinders and tablets holding a bucket.

According to the "Book of Ramadosh," the "Bucket" contained the elixir of life. And in secret ritual ceremonies held on the Island of Arwad, Ugarit, Tyre, Sidon, Byblos and inside the Temple of Solomon, and the palace of Hiram, drops of water from the "Bucket" were used as Za'apharan, a sort of a yellowish writing ink, invisible to the naked eye. Such practice was not part of magical rituals, but prescriptions of secret extraterrestrial techniques which developed supernatural powers.

The Za'apharan was also used in the early Arabian magic ceremonies and spirits séances, to write down the secret and powerful names of Allah (The Muslim God), the Al Arwah (The spirits), and the Jinns.

The divine names were written on a magical circle drawn on the floor, and/or waxed parchment-papers. The word Za'apharan is not a linguistic fantasy. It did exist in the ancient literature of the Near East and the Middle East.

As a matter of fact, Za'apharan is still use in many modern Eastern languages, including Turkish, Persian, Arabic and Syriac (Syriani).

***   ***   ***

77. A tool to Rewind the Past and the Future
"Lamada-burkadi"
⌘ ⌘ ⌘

Definition:
An instrument that functions and operates as a camera and a projector. It has a lens and two knobs; one for rewinding the past, the other for projecting the future.
It works like this: It projects events that have occurred in the past, yet these events were captured by the lens of the camera existing in the future.

***   ***   ***

78. Metaphysical Visual Stethoscope "Lamadru"
⌘⌘⌘

Definition:
Ulema de Lafayette compared it to a "metaphysical visual stethoscope", used to measure the distance between a physical body and the "Double".
One of its functions is to restore health, and equilibrium between the physical and the mental.

***   ***   ***

79. Announcement of your Death "Latabi" "Ma-ari" ⌘⌘⌘

I. Definition
II. Ulema Al Baydani explains

I. Definition:
A term for the experience of encountering or seeing yourself, as a duplicate image of your body. Some Ulema reluctantly called this phenomenon "Announcement of your death."

II. Ulema Al Baydani explains:
Ulema Al Baydani commented on this. He said verbatim:
- This is not a good sign.
- Usually the projection of the image of one's body predicts either a fatal event to occur in the very near future, or his/her death within hours or a few days.
- Pets can easily see this image.
- It is not physical, however it appears very clear to the naked eye.
- The image takes the form of a ghost looking at you.
- The ghost moves like a real person.
- Usually you see confusion and sadness on the face of the ghost.
- This is not hallucination or a trick of your mind.
- It is a holographic projection of an event to occur.
- In other words, your mind (The Supersymetric Mind) can sense and pre-visualize events before they happen.
- It is like reading a calendar backward; from the end, instead from the very first day of the month.
- It is a rare occurrence, but it happens now and then.

80. The Image of the Bodies of People Who Have Passed Away
"Lakur-bashar-shabah"
"Mah.Ga.Ri"
⌘⌘⌘

I. Definition
II. Etymology

I. Definition:
The projection of the images of the bodies of people who have passed away. Yet, at a certain time interval, in an adjacent parallel dimension, the continuity of their physical existence is a real, as the one they had while still alive on earth.

II. Etymology:
Worth mentioning here that:
- **1-** Bashar is an Anunnaki word for humans. Bashar was one of the primordial words, the Anunnaki geneticists used to refer to their genetic creatures. These creatures were the prototype of the first human beings. More precisely, the first quasi-human creatures. In addition to Bashar, other names were used, such Adama, Ada-mah, Naffar, etc.
- **2-** The word Shabah means ghost or phantom in Arabic. It is still used in the Arabic language, and particularly in the Arabic Sihr (Arabic Magic) literature.

In its Anunnaki-Ulemite original context, Shabah meant the etheric energy diffused by your physical body. It could be seen as a real entity in the "next dimension", the one that follows the third dimension which is Earth.

On Earth, Shabbah resembles Latabi, but after the event of one' death has occurred.

81. Reappearance of Objects Which Are No Longer in Existence
Lakur-shabah"
"Mah.Ri.Nag"
⌘ ⌘ ⌘

I. Definition
II. Etymology

I. Definition:
Lakur-shabah is a term or a word for a place or an object that has existed once upon a time, but it seems to reappear somehow, somewhere to some people. Such a place could be an old street, a shop from another century, etc.
An object could be a ship from the old times, an archeological statue, or even the face of a deity.

II. Etymology:
Lakur-shabah is composed of three words:

- **a**-La, which means no. (Same meaning in Sumerian, Akkadian, Assyrian, proto-Aramaic, and Arabic.)
- **b**-Kur, which means a place, a land, a field, a region. (Same meaning in Sumerian, Akkadian, Assyrian and Old Babylonian.)
- **c**-Shabah, which means a ghost. (Same meaning in Arabic.)

*** *** ***

NOTES

NOTES

NOTES

NOTES

PRINTED IN THE UNITED STATES OF AMERICA

Made in the USA
Las Vegas, NV
20 October 2022